Motion
Graphics

100 Design
Projects You
Can't Miss

Edited by Wang Shaoqiang

promopress

Motion Graphics

100 Design Projects
You Can't Miss

Editor: Wang Shaoqiang
English preface revised by: Tom Corkett

Copyright © 2017 by Sandu Publishing Co., Ltd.
Copyright © 2017 English language edition by
Promopress for sale in Europe and America.
Promopress is a brand of:
Promotora de Prensa Internacional S.A.
C/ Ausiàs March, 124
08013 Barcelona, Spain
Phone: 0034 93 245 14 64
Fax: 0034 93 265 48 83
info@promopress.es
www.promopresseditions.com
Facebook: Promopress Editions
Twitter: Promopress Editions @PromopressEd
Sponsored by Design 360°
– Concept and Design Magazine
Edited and produced by
Sandu Publishing Co., Ltd.
Book design, concepts & art direction by
Sandu Publishing Co., Ltd.
info@sandupublishing.com

Cover design: wearebold.es

ISBN: 978-84-16851-29-4
D.L.: B-17264-2017

Printed in China

Contents

Preface

Hugo Moss

The founder of Huge Designs,
An Emmy Award Winning Titles Design Company

Ever since I started my career in titles design twenty-five years ago, people have never stopped asking me what I do for a living. I always used to dread having to explain to them what a titles designer does. I would say that we do not simply pick a font randomly and type people's names. But at that time, it seemed that titles design and motion design were not in people's psyche.

Twenty-five years later, I do not flinch when people ask me the same question. Instead, I get excited when telling them what I am working on. Motion graphics and titles design are now a "thing." Titles designers' nights are filled with producing immersive sequences for their favourite series that will be shown before, during, and even after the show is broadcast. And influential awards like the Emmys and the BAFTAS explain to the public how creatives artistically convey themes, ideas, and values using the power of storytelling. College courses that cover the field are oversubscribed because of the ranks of enthusiastic and talented creatives who see motion graphics as their future.

Motion graphics is now an exciting business with plenty of room for creativity and originality. Something new emerges in the field every year. A new trend will ripple out across the industry and become the language of titles for a while. For example, back in the nineties, Kyle Cooper's *Se7en* titles once ushered in a new era in titles design, and afterwards there would be a game changer in the field every few years.

As a designer, I could not be happier to be in this world. Every brief is original, and every solution that we come up with is totally refreshing. You will never get bored if you are a titles designer. It is a bit like being a bespoke tailor. First, you must look at what the titles will be for, how they will be used, and what the story will portray. With all the answers in hand, you start to cut the cloth. The crucial thing is to please the customer, but at the same time it is important to add stylistic elements that make each project unique and distinguished. You have to be the master of everything and have a good command of colour, typography, animation, and timing.

You must also be aware of trends and keep ahead of them. The most exciting part of the job is that every story is different. Motion graphics designers have a lot of tools at their disposal. Some opening credits — for example, those for *Downton Abbey* — only need beautiful live action shots accompanied by delicate typography. But for other projects, you might find yourself filming someone swinging from the ceiling against a green screen, as we had to do for *By Any Means*. A sequence's key visuals could have you doing anything, from setting fire to props to pouring ink into water or climbing onto the roof to film a time-lapse sky. You may even work with more traditional techniques. For example, to make the titles for *Da Vinci's Demons*, we produced sketches on paper, and these were then scanned and overlaid on live action shots.

The beauty of motion graphics is that the software used to make them, which is now extremely accessible, has no boundaries or limitations. With up-to-date technology, you can unveil a beautiful new world to your audience, anytime and anywhere. You can create these worlds without leaving your design studio or bedroom. You can even produce material for a feature film on a laptop while sitting on a train. What matters most in motion design are not physical limitations, but rather imagination, execution, and cooperation.

As cutting-edge technology plays such an important role in this area, people may wonder how the art of motion graphics will evolve. With the viral nature of the Internet, a project can be seen as soon as it is released. And the aspiration to be original stimulates graphic designers to experiment ceaselessly. The evolution of this domain has the potential to be remarkable, and probably unlike any other art form, new motion design pieces consistently create surprise.

The software and hardware used in the industry are rapidly evolving. Tracking software was once only available on high-end machinery, but nowadays it is accessible to all. Compositing software now comes bundled with free 3D applications; drones can be found everywhere; and cameras shoot faster and produce images in much higher resolutions than they ever did before. We are in the midst of an age when the evolution of technology shows no sign of slowing down.

Despite this technological arms race, designers can still innovate in a simple yet experimental way. You might be one of those designers whose studio time is spent crashing, bashing, burning, and melting; or you might prefer painting, cutting, tearing, or simply making a mess. All these approaches share a single objective: the creation of new textures and emotions on camera.

However, one simple thing ultimately matters above all else: the design is everything. It is a principle that can be found throughout this volume, which showcases an amazingly diverse range of projects. Every page is unique and fresh. The projects revealed here have been created by designers who are at the top of their game and who continuously develop new visual languages and break boundaries. The book itself is also a breakthrough, as it presents a young art form that is at the very beginning of its development.

The examples on the pages that follow have been carefully selected, and they could be considered as the cream of what the global industry is producing right now. May they inspire you and encourage you to keep pushing the boundaries, to carry on experimenting, and to pursue the next new thing.

"
The evolution of this domain has
the potential to be remarkable,
and probably unlike any other art form,
new motion design pieces
consistently create surprise.
"

Commercial

▶ Boeing 100

by Loop

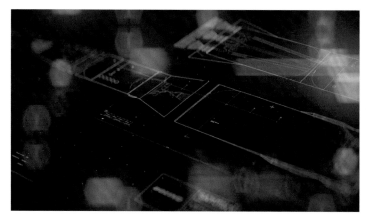

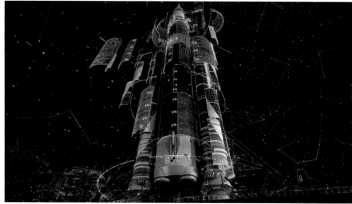

Agency
FCB

Production & VFX
Aggressive, Loop

Creative Direction
Alex Topaller, Dan Shapiro,
Alex Mikhaylov

Executive Production
Dan Shapiro

Art Direction & Design
Alex Mikhaylov

CG Supervision
Max Chelyadnikov

Modelling
E.D.Satan, Valentine Sorokin,
Roman Senko

2D Animation
Vladimir Tomin, Alex Frukta

3D Animation
Dmitriy Paukov, Roman Senko

Editing
Dan Shapiro, Alex Mikhaylov

FX TD
Nikolay Lvov, Daniil Rybkin

Matte Painting
Dmitriy Ten

Rendering
Max Chelyadnikov

Composition
Max Chelyadnikov,
Roman Senko

Production Management
Dustin Pownal

Storyboard Art
Anton Antonov

Sound Design
Wesley Slover

Sound Design (Dir Cut)
Echoic

Client
Boeing

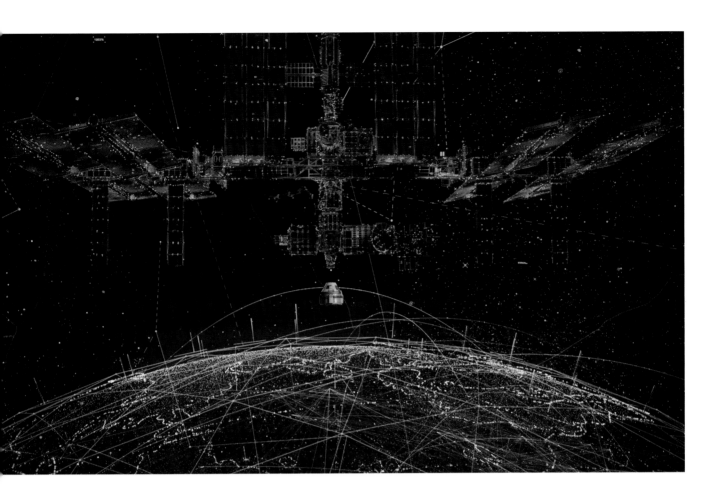

This film is one of the three spots to celebrate Boeing's 100th anniversary. Executed by seamless design and hyper-real CG, they drew inspiration from engineering blueprints. Each spot captures the awe-inspiring process that starts with a single spark in the mind of a Boeing engineer, and finishes with a gravity defying roar of an engine which takes a machine to unprecedented altitudes.

It perfectly blurs the line between imagination and reality, showcasing Boeing's ambitious spirit to adventure the unknown regime. The use of colour, the instant installation from components to the rocket, and the following smart transition from blueprints to a real object generate a hi-tech feel, exemplifying human's everlasting pursuit of advanced technology and adventurous minds.

Vimeo **Official**

▶ Mercedes-Benz Clientele Film
by Panoply

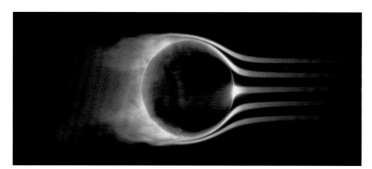 

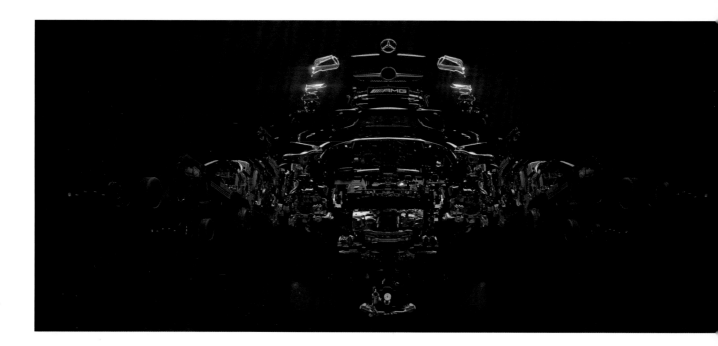

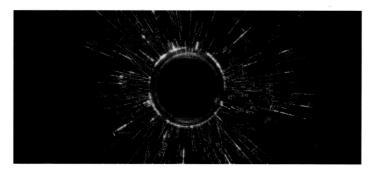 

Design
Renaud Futterer, Mark Lindner,
Damian Sendin

Audio
Echoic Audio

Client
Raid Films, Atelier Markgraph

Panoply was approached by RAID Films and Atelier Markgraph to create the initial piece in a series of films for Mercedes-Benz, focusing on the production and manufacture of their vehicles. The film has five manufacturing concepts that were outlined by Raid and Atelier — safety, perfection, quality, precision, and awakening. These initial brand values were brought together to drive the abstract visual thread that runs throughout the film.

Vimeo **Official**

▶ The New Generation of Home Appliances
by Ouchhh Studio

Sound Design
Audiofil

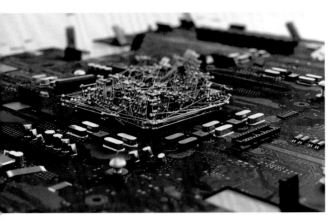

Ouchhh Studio animated this film to explore the new forms
of technology and to re-define the new generation of
Home Appliances.

Vimeo   **Official**

▶ Pomellato / Sabbia

by Ditroit

Direction
Alex Tacchi

Art Direction
Salvatore Giunta,
Pietro Furbatto

Design
Salvatore Giunta,
Pietro Furbatto

Modelling
Giovanni Mauro

Lighting & Shading
Salvatore Giunta,
Pietro Furbatto

3D Animation
Pietro Furbatto, Daniela Zanne

Composition
Salvatore Giunta,
Pietro Furbatto

Music & Sound Design
Smider

Author
Guia Ciceri,
Andrea Bempensante, Otto Bell

Speaker
Emma Powell

Client
Pomellato

SABBIA

For the Pomellato Icon Movies project, Ditroit was among the three Italian directors that were invited to express their own artistic interpretation of three of the Pomellato's icon jewels. The Sabbia Ring was their object of interest and they imagined a dreamlike space-time trip through precious minerals and stones, ending on the shimmering surface of the ring.

Vimeo   **Official**

▶ Jaguar I-Pace
by Frame

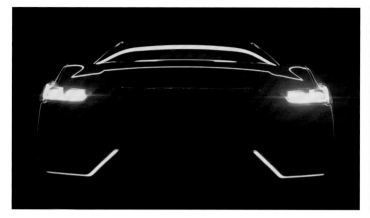
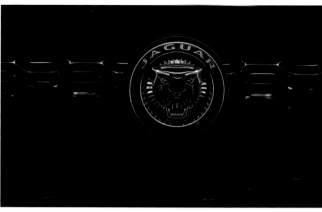
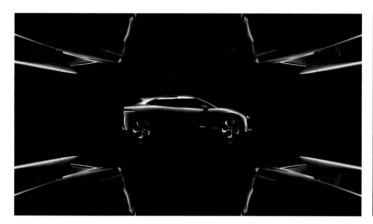

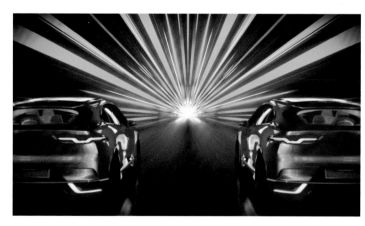

Concept & Post Production
Frame

Production Company
Dirty Films

Direction
Tom Crate (Frame)

Executive Production
Thomas Bay (Frame)

Creative Direction
Anders Schroder (Frame)

Direction of Photography
Bernd Wondollek

Colouring
Denny Cooper (Rushes)

Composition
Ryan West (Rival Consoles)

Sound Design
750 MPH

Record Label
Erased Tapes

Engineer
Mark Hellaby

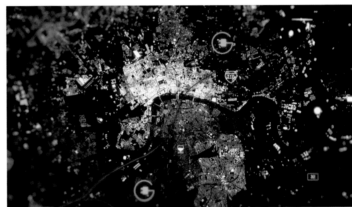

Collaborating with Dirty Films and agency Spark 44 London, the film reveals features of the car and it is a noteworthy design through an alluring, infinitely zooming world, which pushed Frame to explore the limitation of a commercial spot for a car.

Their primary inspiration was the White Stripes music video "Seven Nation Army." They wanted the journey to be hypnotic and relentless, evoking feelings of forward motion as if being carried by the smooth but powerful electric engine from Jaguar. They wanted to create an "infinite zoom" effect where the entire film becomes a seamless trip through the formation of the new electric car from Jaguar.

As they travel through a universe comprised of kaleidoscopic tunnels of light and abstract shapes, features of the car become more detailed and defined with the car's geography being unravelled.

Vimeo   **Official**

▶ Sport FM

by Loop

 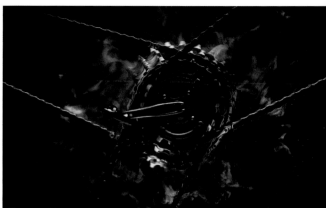

Direction
Alex Mikhaylov

Art Direction
Alex Mikhaylov

CG Supervision
Max Chelyadnikov

Modelling
Dmitriy Paukov,
Max Chelyadnikov

Animation
Dmitriy Paukov

Rendering
Max Chelyadnikov

FX
Alexey Komarov,
Valdemaras Dzengo

Composition
Max Chelyadnikov

Client
Sport FM

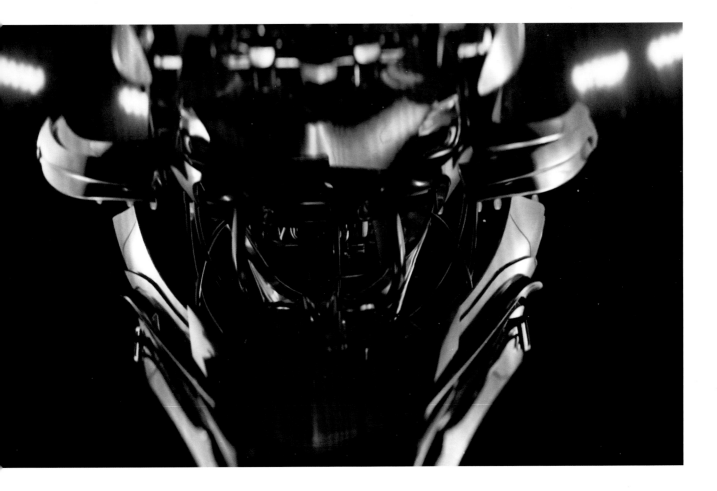

It is a commercial spot for Sport FM. Beginning with a rotating gear in an increasing speed, this film showcases various sports accessories with a mechanical transition, creating a match-like hyper tense atmosphere.

Vimeo   **Official**

► BMW TVC "Sustainability"

by Goodbye Kansas

Agency
Lowe Brindfors

Direction
Fredrik Löfberg

VFX Production
Hanna Bengtsson

Art Direction
Rickard Engqvist

VFX Supervision
Henrik Eklundh

Rigging
Peter Jemstedt, Jonas Ekman,
Simon Rainerson

Look Dev
Henrik Eklundh, Jonas Skoog,
Daniel Bystedt

Animation
Jonas Ekman, Rickard Engqvist,
Gustav Alexandersson

FX
Simon Rainerson

Lighting
Henrik Eklundh

Composition
Calle Granström

Modelling
Daniel Bystedt, Jonas Skoog,
Erik Tylberg, Max Wikdahl,
Jonas Ekman

Note
Winner of Best Animation
Award at Roy Award 2015

HÅLLBARHET
PÅ VÄG.

FRÅN DEN LEDANDE BILTILLVERKAREN PÅ HÅLLBARHET
I DOW JONES SUSTAINABILITY INDEX 9 ÅR AV 10.

När du älskar
att köra

In order to highlight their environmental focus, BMW commissioned Goodbye Kansas to design a promotion video. Their idea was to depict a world where everything was made of recycled materials. They strived to employ visual approaches that made this recycled world seem physical, like a miniature world with a big heart.

Vimeo   Official

▶ Bundesliga — GFX 2015

by 4HUMANS

Direction
Facu Labo

The German Football League reached out to 4HUMANS to produce, direct, and animate all the graphics used for their 2015 international and local transmissions.

The video is composed of 3 single projects, respectively "International Opener, " "Forever: Video on Demand, " and "Bundesliga Season Shows." Centred on a football team striving for a goal, they created undefined players with their shirts changing from the 16 football teams of the Bundesliga. The smooth and skilful dribbling and moves showcase the excitement of the league. Low poly 3D techniques and particles explode all over the place while the players make super cool moves!

Vimeo   Official

▶ Samsung GearS2 Classic

by MAINCONCEPT

Creative Direction
Taiho Roh

Art Direction
Taiho Roh

Motion Graphic Design
Taiho Roh, Rae Hyuk Park

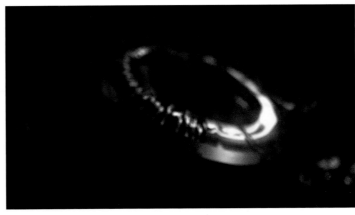

The project was designed to introduce Samsung's new smart Watch GearS2. Most of the existing smart watches are square frames. The design of the gear S2 maintains a circular frame to express the intrinsic value of a classical watch.

In order to take ownership of the circular frame, the film put emphasis on its shape with fascinating rotation and transformation, letting the circle unveil its charm.

Vimeo   **Official**

▶ Volvo S90

by Radugadesign

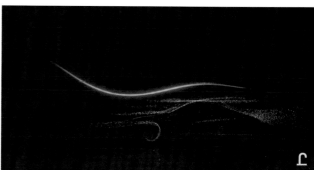

АРХИТЕКТУРА
МАСШТАБИРУЕМОЙ
ПЛАТФОРМЫ **SPA**

Design Agency
Radugadesign, Avantgarde

Creative Direction
Mikhail Kabatov, Ivan Nefedkin

Production
Tanya Sopp

**Direction of
CG Production**
Roman Goobanov

Concept Art
Sergey Voronov

Lead CG Generalist
Elen Elkiev

CG Generalist
Artur Zhamaletdinov,
Dmitry Kulikov

Sound FX
Veniamin Rayev

**Technical Direction of
The Show**
Vitaliy Erzikov

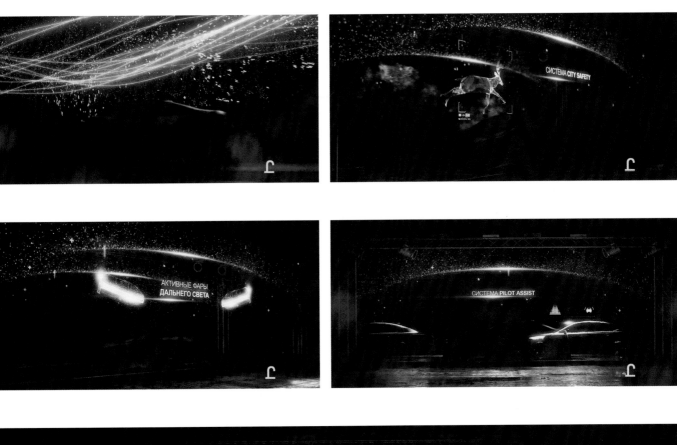

With the help of holographic projections, Radugadesign created an illusion of a protective dome all over the car, by which reflected the company's values — safety and comfort. Also, they managed to transmit the technological features and ideas that inspired the creators of the Volvo S90 model.

Vimeo   **Official**

▶ flygresor.se
by Goodbye Kansas

Agency
Robert German

Agency Production
Fabian Mannheimer

Production Company
Goodbye Kansas

Direction
Rickard Engqvist

CG Supervision
Daniel Bystedt,
Johan Gabrielsson

Comp Lead
Karl Rydhe

Production
Johan Edström,
Hanna Bengtsson

Executive Production
Claes Dietmann

Concept & Artwork
Rickard Engqvist,
Gustav Ekelund,
Martin Bergquist,
Victor Norman

CG Art
Joel Sundberg,
Gustav Alexandersson,
Erik Hallberg, Rodrigo Vivedes,
Jonas Skoog, Peter Jemstedt,
Agnes Lindsten, Joakim Olsson,
Sean Kalamgi, David Enbom,
Hannes Drossel, Kristian Zarins,
Raoul Cacciamani,
Fredrik Olsson, Jonas Forsman,
Christina Sidoti,
Alexis Andersson,
Henrik Klein, Hannah Myllyoja,
Denys Holovyanko,
Sven Ahlström,

Martin Borell, Zebastian Lilja,
Fredrik Mannerfelt,
Max Wester, Tomas Näslund,
Calle Granström

Pipeline
Erik Johansson,
Emil Ferdinandsson

The Swedish online travel agency flygresor.se is well known for commercials involving catchy songs and cute kittens. For their new commercial, they approached Goodbye Kansas to create a new visual style. The result is a world of paper and imagination.

Vimeo   Official

▶ Tata T1 Prima Truck Racing Championship Show Opener

by Sagnik Sengupta

 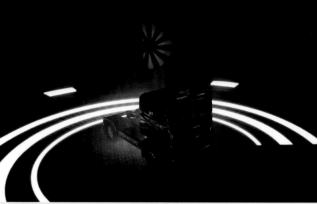

Design Agency
Ten Sports Network

Music
Fearless Motivation

This was a show opener done for Tata Truck Racing Championship 2016 for Ten Sports Network which was held at India's globally renowned F1 race track — the Buddh International Circuit (BIC), Greater Noida.

The concept was to reveal the truck slowly and give it a grand look. The environment was kept dark mostly to focus on the truck with footage screens running at the back to give an idea what the event is all about. The base model of the truck was downloaded and textured accordingly.

Vimeo **Official**

▶ Fendi Jungle Collection

by Ditroit

Art Direction
Salvatore Giunta,
Pietro Furbatto

Design
Salvatore Giunta,
Pietro Furbatto,
Cristian Acquaro,
Andrea Stragapede

Modelling
Giovanni Mauro,
Pietro Furbatto

Lighting & Shading
Salvatore Giunta,
Pietro Furbatto,
Alberto Blasi

Rigging
Cristian Acquaro,
Giovanni Mauro

Animation
Cristian Acquaro,
Andrea Stragapede

Composition
Salvatore Giunta

Music & Sound Design
Smider

Agency
Withstand

Executive Production
Davide Ferazza

Production
Ilaria Celeghin

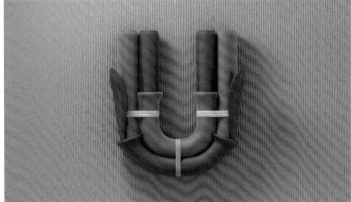

Fendi commissioned Ditroit to design a product video for
their new collection of sunglasses, requesting the product
to be placed in a jungle inspired environment. Ditroit used
JUNGLE both as the title and as an inspiration for the concept
behind this video.

Vimeo   **Official**

▶ Biggerpan

by Mikhail Sedov

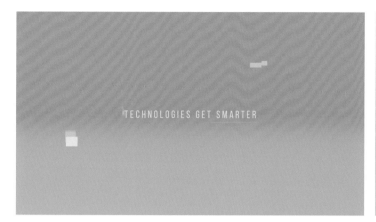

Agency
Moose Tank

Idea
Moose Tank

Creative Direction
Moose Tank

Art Direction
Mikhail Sedov, Paul Shtyler

Render & Composition
Mikhail Sedov

Motion Art
Vasiliy Filileev, Mikhail Sedov

Music & Sound Design
Dmitry Balakin

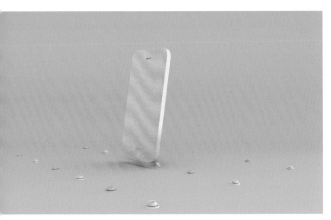

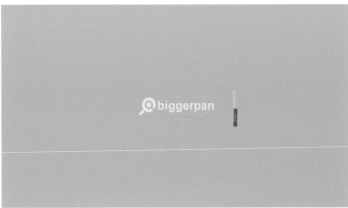

Ever since the web was created, the most relevant content has always been a time-consuming process, if not a challenging routine. With a truly innovative approach to content discovery and search, the technology by Moose Tank brings real-time and automation for the first time on the client side. Biggerpan also adds context to enhance visitors' experience and give them a better guidance. In short, they save time. This film concisely introduces this technology in a funny way.

Vimeo   **Official**

▶ Acers RGB & Rec. 709 For Digital Displays Explained

by Chu-Chieh Lee

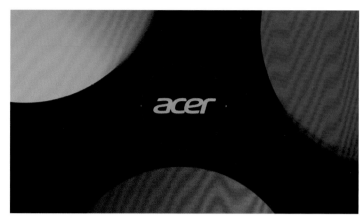

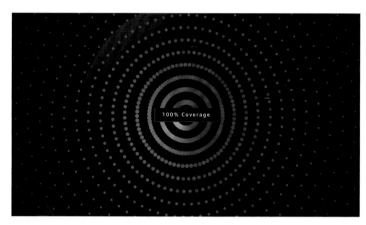
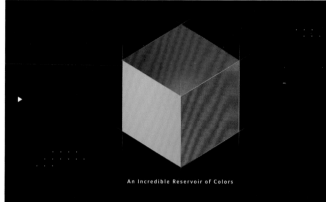

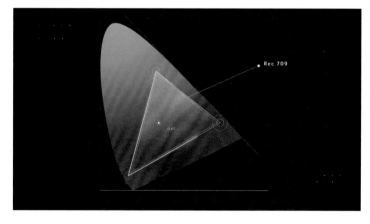
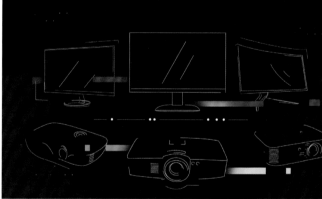

Production
MoonShine VFX

Direction
Chu-Chieh Lee

Production
Yeh Chuan Yao

Design
Chu-Chieh Lee, Chuan-Yao Yeh

2D Animation
Phil Wu, Bruce Chen,
Chu-Chieh Lee

3D Animation
Phil Wu

Music & Sound Design
Hsiao-Chin Lin, Szu-yu Lin
(WinSound Studio)

**Scoring Mix &
Re-recording Mix**
Hsiao-Chin Lin

Client
Acer

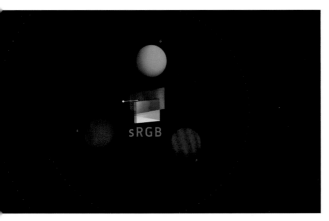

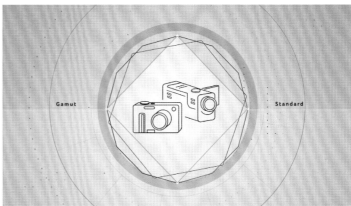

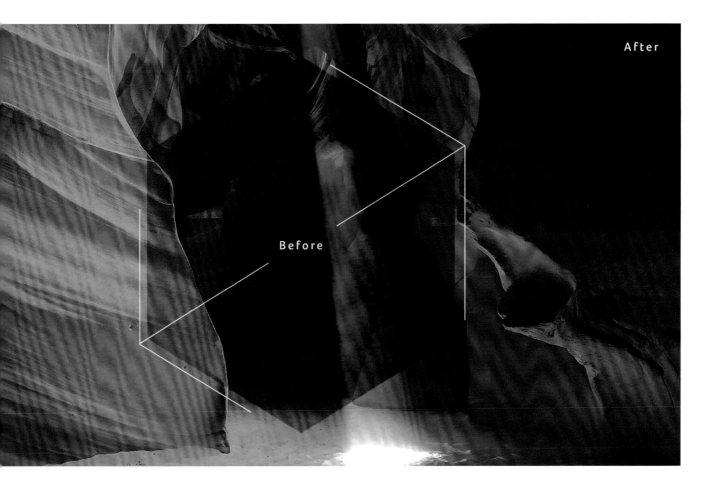

Introducing Acer & Rec. 709 solution on display, the video explains how their displays could deliver high colour accuracy by reaching wider colour gamut include sRGB & Rec. 709. With these standards, customers could easily enjoy the accurate and consistent reproduction of colour through Acer's displays.

Vimeo   **Official**

▶ Absolut
by Ouchhh Studio

Sound Design
Audiofil

ABSOLUT.

Non-commercial work using Absolut's iconic bottle.

As salute to Absolut's iconic bottle, Ouchhh Studio has transformed it to show many of its characteristics, flavours and possible new designs by creating abstract and surreal bottle designs in a photo-realistic way. They used the Absolut bottle as a dummy for this design practice and created the video by combining scenes from their daily renders at Ouchhh.

Vimeo   Official

▶ Panthella Mini

by Frame

 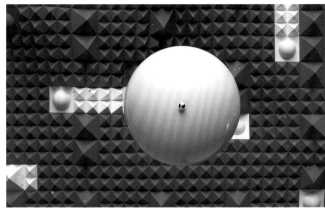

 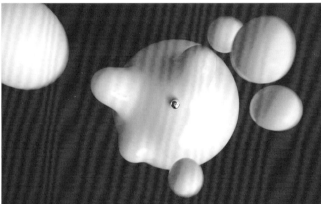

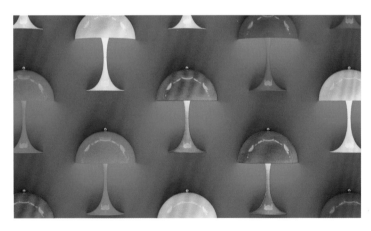 

Direction
Matias Hansen

Creative Direction
Anders Schroder

Executive Production
Thomas Bay

Design
Matias Hansen

Animation
Filip Kobjevski,
Matias Hansen, Aske Westh,
Sacha Wechselmann

Sound Design
Zelig Sound

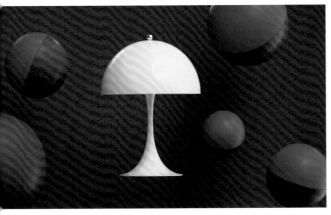
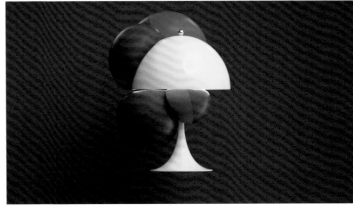

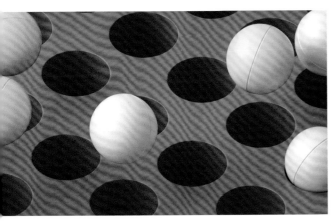
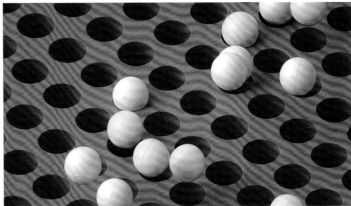

louis poulsen

Panthella MINI

Design: Verner Panton

Vejl. udsalgspris
kr. 2.795

shop.louispoulsen.dk

louis poulsen

Design to Shape Light

The "Panthella Mini" lamp is a smaller version of the original Panthella lamp, launched in 1971. The Panthella Mini features a metal shade and comes in 11 delicious colours. The legendary Danish designer Verner Panton is known for his use of powerful colours, organic shapes, and unconventional materials.

As a starting point, Frame investigated Panton's aesthetic universe and commenced designing a tour de force of lamps, eye popping colours and abstract shapes, inspired by the man himself. They were also encouraged by Louis Poulsen to give it their own personal touch so they had the freedom to interpret the unique style of Verner Panton with a unique twist and establish a lighter, more contemporary tone. In the end, it was all about creating something warm, happy, alive, intelligent and playful, just like Panton himself, a setting for the lamps to shine (no pun intended) and allow the focus to remain on these beautifully designed objects.

Vimeo   Official

► Emporio Armani Watches & Jewelry Collection

by Ditroit

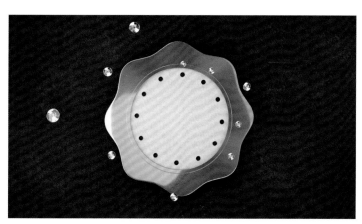

**Art Direction &
Set Design**
Salvatore Giunta

Modelling
Giovanni Mauro,
Enrico Albanese

Lighting & Shading
Claudio Gasparollo

Animation
Cristian Acquaro

Music & Sound Design
Smider

Agency
Lorenzo Banal

Client
Armani

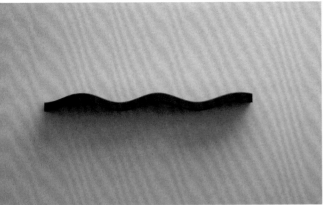
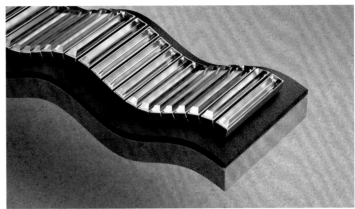

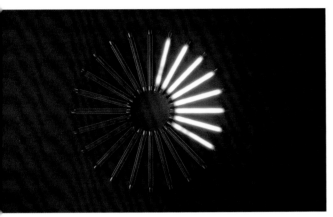

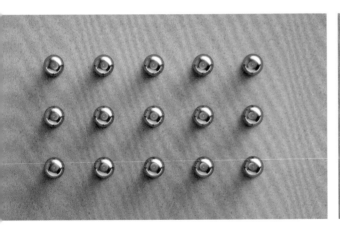

For this Emporio Armani product video, Ditroit identified several graphic elements on each product of the collection and that was the starting point for the entire concept. The designers tried to stay true to the shapes and textures of the very products, emphasizing at the same time their design and aesthetics.

Vimeo   **Official**

▶ SM Station

by Cobb Studio

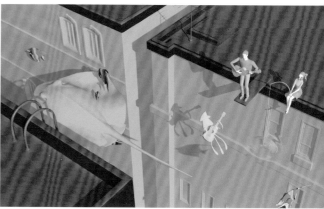

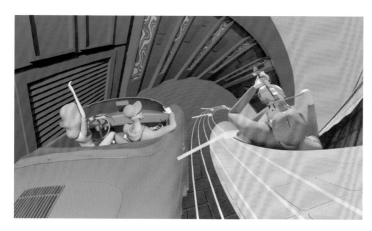

Direction
Eunjin Cho

Animation
Wonseok Lee, Cheolhoon Ahn,
Hyunjung Yoo

Design
Shinyoung Kim, Eugene Lee

SM Station is an open channel of SM Entertainment that releases new music every Friday. Their goal is to collaborate with various artists, producers, composers, and other companies and create diversity in music.

In order to effectively present this concept, Cobb Studio used two colours in each scene to show how two different worlds are met to create unique scenes. Also each scene is designed to represent different genres of music, connected by smooth transitions from beginning to end.

Vimeo   **Official**

▶ Moneyfarm
by Illo

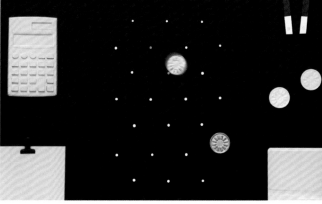

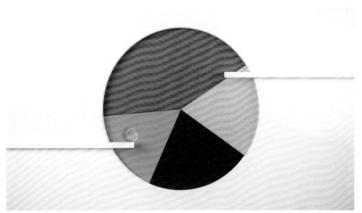
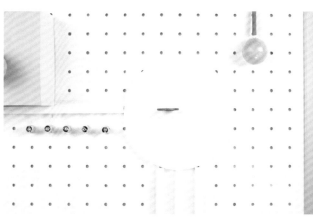

YOUR DEDICATED
INVESTMENT
CONSULTANT

√ A PORTFOLIO MATCHED
TO YOUR PROFILE

√ A TEAM WORKING
FOR YOU

Direction & Set Design
Ilenia Notarangelo

Post Prod & Animation
Miriam Palopoli

Direction & Post Prod
Luca Gonnelli

Post Prod
Matteo Ruffinengo,
Laurentiu Lunic

Props & Sound Design
Carla Gioia

Set design, also known as tactile design or tangible design, is a powerful trend combining the beauty of real life scenarios with the typical abstraction of illustrations.

Approaching this work for Moneyfarm, which is part of a campaign made of six videos plus one, Illo tried to bring a tangible aspect — coins running through an incredible machine — to an investment process which is completely digital and runs exclusively online.

Vimeo   Official

▶ Together as One

by Le Cube

 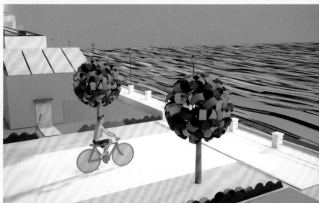

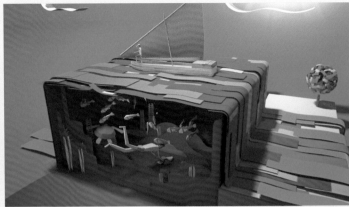

ooredoo.com

Ooredoo commissioned Le Cube to create a commercial film to promote their new strategy "Together as One." For this international telecommunications company headquartered in Doha, Le Cube created a world in paper-model style, interpreting the concept in a cosy style.

Vimeo   **Official**

▶ Coachademy

by Illo

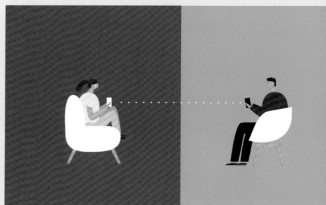

Creative Direction
Ilenia Notarangelo

Illustration
Cristina Pasquale

Copywriting
Claudia Losini

Animation
Nicholas Bertini

Sound Design
Carla Gioia

Client
coachademy.com

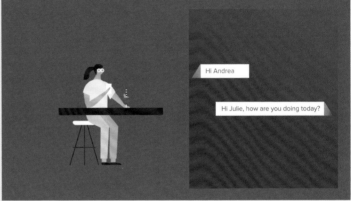

Coachademy is a new personal consultant app. Illo designed this concept video to promote this not yet available product to its target audiences. A series of catchy illustrations were created for this video which can be redeployed for other media, such as website, social channels, and presentations.

Vimeo   **Official**

▶ Branca Menta — Avanzá
by 4HUMANS

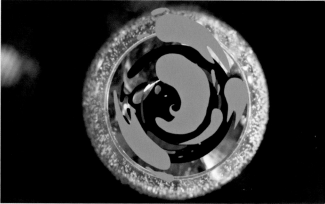

Direction
Flamboyant Paradise

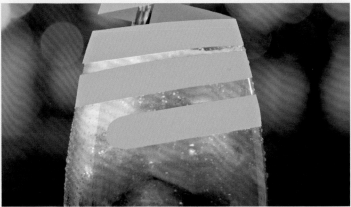

Together with Flamboyant Paradise, 4HUMANS created a strong colour palette for this 2D animated commercial film for Branca Menta. This nocturnal trip took place between the moment when Branca Menta first comes into contact with the ice and the effervescent moment when it bubbles up to the edge of the glass, ready to be enjoyed.

The narrative brings in a fancy imagination realized by fluid-alike transitions between different scenes, enchanting illustrated characters, and the imaginary exciting shows in the club atmosphere, illustrating the dizzy yet delightful moments with this tasteful drink.

Vimeo   **Official**

▶ LINCOLN CONTINENTAL
by Block & Tackle

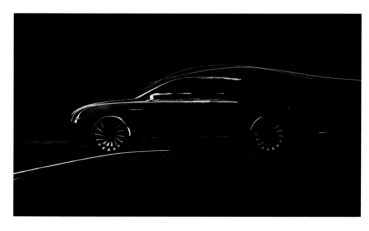 

Creative Direction
Ted Kotsaftis, Adam Gault

Production
Michael Neithardt

Art Direction
Gordon Waltho

Project Lead
William Huang

Animation
Ted Kotsaftis, Adam Gault,
David Hobizal, Hayato Yamane

Music
Fall On Your Sword

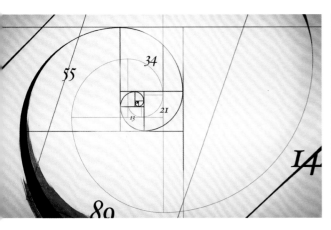
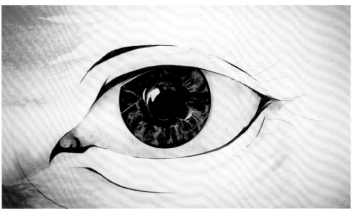

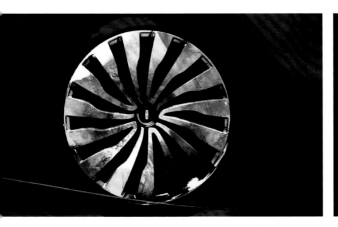

Block & Tackle teamed up with the talented folks at The Lincoln Motor Company and Hudson Rouge to create a tease of the Lincoln Continental Concept car. They started with loose thumbnails of each scene, then designed fully-realized style frames for every moment in the piece and built a tight animatic before animation began. There was a moment in the design phase — when the first style frames were coming together and looking really lush and detailed, but also quite sophisticated — that they realized they were going to have to push the creative limits as much as possible to make sure the animation lived up to the look. The outcome is an homage to travel and exploration, and a tribute to Lincoln's carefully considered approach to designing one of America's most iconic cars.

Vimeo   **Official**

▶ MTV Motor Home

by Ditroit

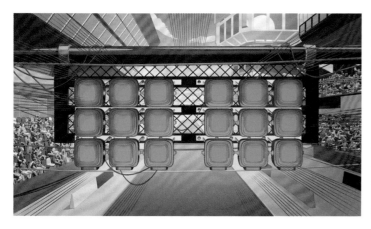

Art Direction
Salvatore Giunta, Luca Dusio

Design
Salvatore Giunta,
Cristian Acquaro

Modelling
Giovanni Mauro,
Daniele Angelozzi

Shading & Lighting
Cristian Acquaro

Rigging
Tommaso Sanguigni

Animation
Cristian Acquaro

2D FX
Jules Guerin

Composition
Salvatore Giunta

Music & Sound Design
Smider

Client
MTV Milano Design Studio

Creative Direction
Lorenzo Banal

Note
Bronze — Bass Awards 2015

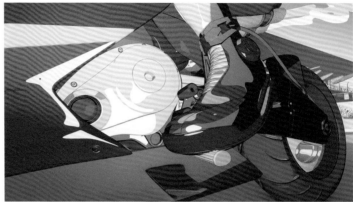

Motor Home was an MTV show about the lives of four young moto riders. In the opener, Ditroit described the adrenaline rush occurring before the start of the race, using a Japanese anime inspired style.

Vimeo   **Official**

▶ The Confidante Miami Hyatt's Hotel

by Le Cube

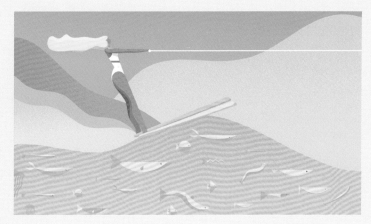 

The Confidante Hotel launched a Twitter competition where people describe their best way to spend 140 hours in Miami. Subsequently, Le Cube's mission was to give life to the best tweet. The soft colours generate a leisure atmosphere for the spot and enlighten the city about its state of being a resort, leading the fancy vacation and bringing in the Hyatt's branding in a subtle way.

Vimeo   Official

▶ So You Wanna be a Fashion Designer

by Daniel Moreno Cordero

Production Company
dreambear

Production
Evan Brown

Commissioned by Brooklyn fashion designer Julie Mojo,
Daniel Moreno Cordero designed and animated this
introduction video for her official website.

Vimeo   Official

▶ Fine Jewellery
by Chu-Chieh Lee

Direction
Chu-Chieh Lee

Production
Ivy Zhuang

Design
Chu-Chieh Lee, How-Yi Chen,
Manning Lee

2D Animation
Chu-Chieh Lee,
Phil Wu, Shumin Wu

Cel Animation
Chu-Chieh Lee, Manning Lee

3D Animation
Chu-Chieh Lee

身为都会时尚新女性

我们每天都想尽善尽美的呈现自己

化为一点善

化为一点善

点钻深信美丽由心而生。
点钻成立1点心意计划回馈社会。

凡于微信平台消费5000元，
点钻会以阁下名义植树一伙。

在收获外在美的同时贡献社会，
还下一代蓝天绿水。

The Video is created for a diamond company based in Hong Kong. The video shows the changes of the environment where people wear the Jewellery of Fine Jewellery's.

The purpose of this video is to convey the main belief of One Heart program that is established by Fine Jewellery. Every tIme the customer purchases the products, they would plant a tree bearing their name. With these design, the video shows the difference before and after people wear the products of Fine Jewellery.

Vimeo   **Official**

▶ Think Minsk

by Alex Frukta

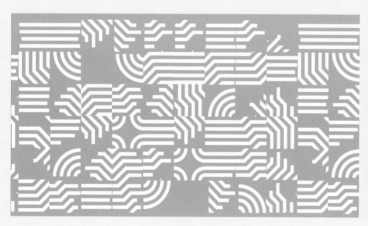 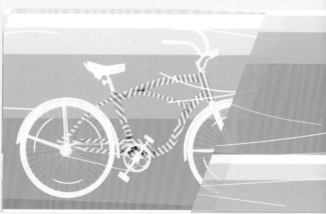

Design Agency
INSTID

Art Direction
Alexander Grand

Design
Maxim Alimkin

Illustration
Maxim Alimkin, Alex Frukta

Motion Direction
Alex Frukta

Voiceover
Ivan Podrez

Score
Yan Maers

© INSTID MMXIII

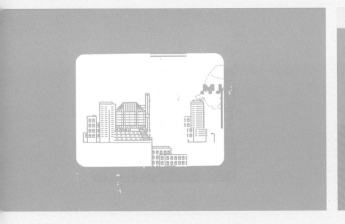

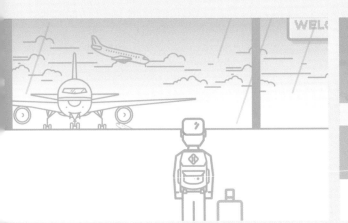

INSTID was asked to help improve international recognition of Minsk to attract foreign investment, visitors, and talent. Within the city itself, the new branding should help residents feel proud of Minsk and develop a unique city culture based on their distinct character, and create a powerful platform for city's future development.

A graphic expression of this archetypal quality of Minsk is delivered by the combination of the light blue colour (the colour of communication, abstract thinking, and intellect) and the line (as a most flexible and effective shape). They designated alternating blue and white stripes of equal width as the key and only imperative for the city visuals and made it open to the Minsk residents, businesses and public bodies for further interpretation and application.

At the end, Brand Minsk has become an original, imaginative and bold solution that not only leaves room for the city's future development, but also gives it direction, energy, and appeal.

Vimeo   **Official**

► MTV "VIDEO LOVE"
by INLAND STUDIO

Art Direction
INLAND STUDIO

Character Design
INLAND STUDIO

Animation
INLAND STUDIO, Matias Sesti

MTV Creative Direction
Nacho Gil MTV

Production
Curtis Conroy MaxDef,
Pat Twist

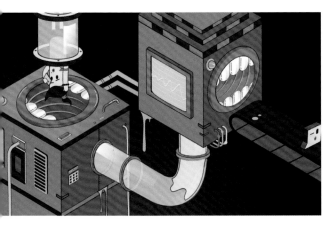
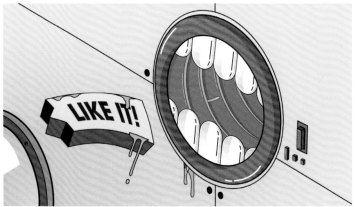

"VIDEO LOVE" is a show that seeks interaction between the screen and the audience. They found fun to play among the humanization of emoticons and "emoticonized" human. This first piece visualized "VIDEO LOVE" as a machine that absorbs people and their comments, and converts them into emoticons that feed the great machine.

Vimeo   **Official**

▶ Apparat

by Alex Frukta

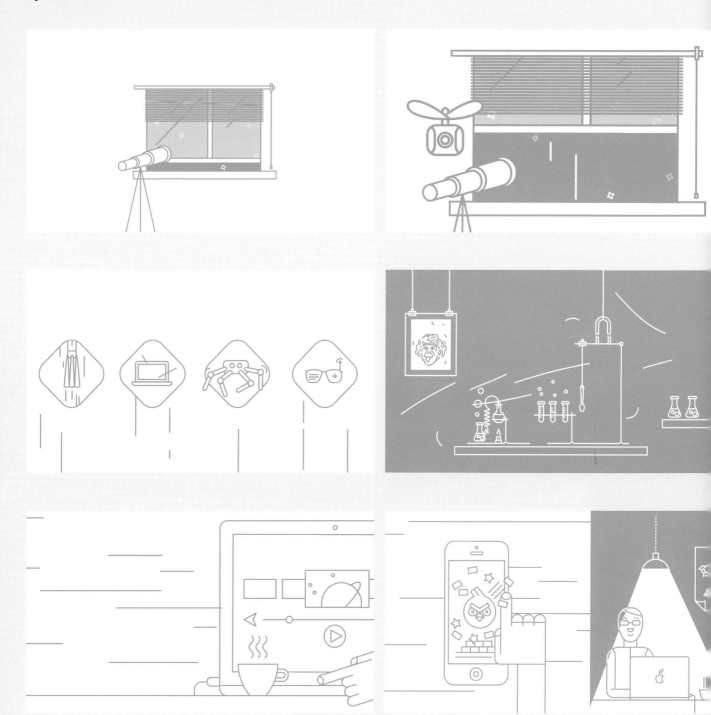

Design
Ooli Mos, Alexey Frukta

Production
Artem Ignatyev

Audio
Vasiliy Filatov

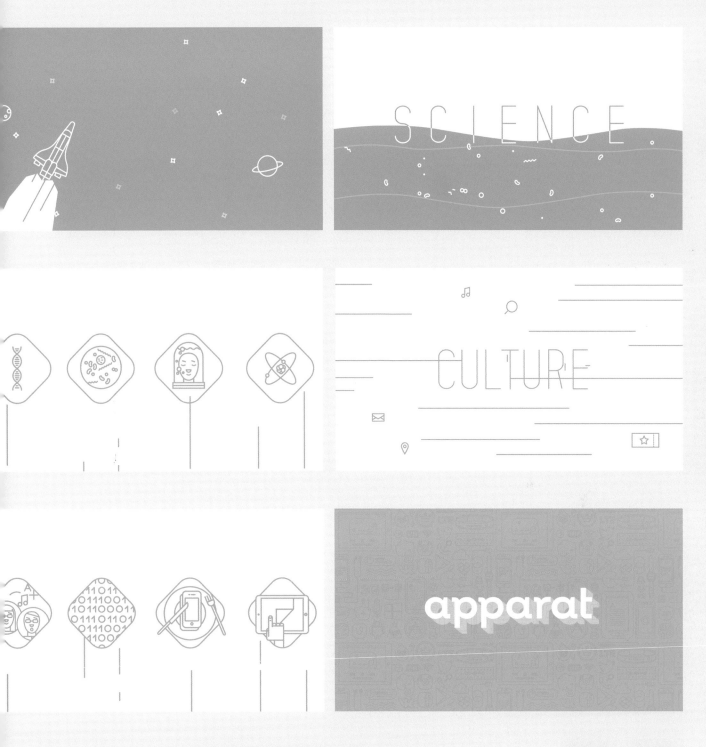

Apparat is a new Russian daily online magazine for people who are interested in the technology, science, and culture. The magazine covers topics such as the influence of modern technology on society, consequences of scientific discoveries, new ethics, the future of technologies, and many others.

Vimeo   **Official**

▶ airbnb app promo

by Sébastien Henau

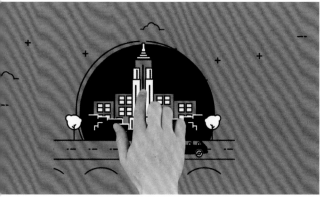
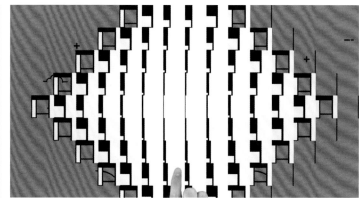

This film was created to be the Final Project for the motion design class. Sébastien Henau was required to choose an A-level brand and make a commercial promoting one of their existing applications with a story and hand gestures.

Vimeo   Official

▶ RCI Banque — Savings Account
by nöbl.tv

 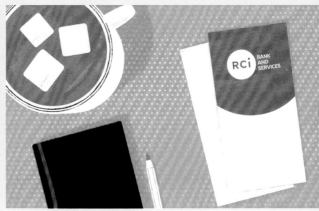

 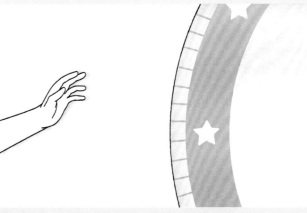

Production
Arpel Films

2D Animation
Faouzi Hammadi

Art Direction & Animation
nöbl

Music
discrete time music

Design
Anna Pirolli

Client
RCI Banque

RCI Bank and Services is a French bank specializing in financing and automotive services of the Renault-Nissan brands.

RCI Bank and Services launched its saving product with ZESTO & PEPITO, safe and performing in France. The proceeds are reinvested in the distribution of car loans for the Renault-Nissan brands.

Vimeo   **Official**

Cultural

▶ TEDxCERN

by Ouchhh Studio

Sound Design
Audiofil

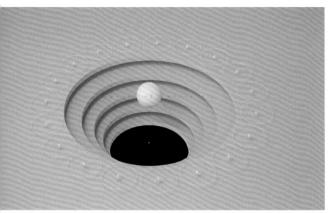 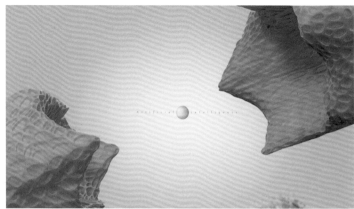

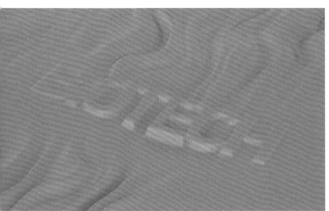 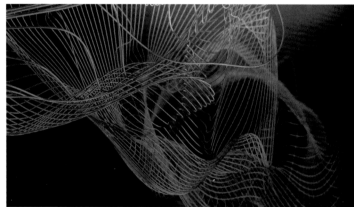

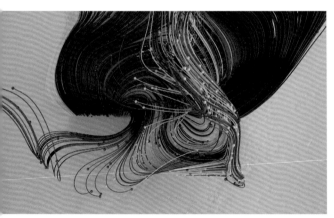 

On November 2016, Ouchhh was invited by CERN to create main title animation for TEDxCERN 2016 event. The title animation was inspired by the event's main theme "ripples of curiosity," where TEDxCERN explored curiosity and innovations it sparks. Topics included artificial intelligence, DNA editing, biotechnology, global literacy, DIY science, drones, oceanography, as well as dark matter and gravitational waves. Ouchhh's science based title animation inspires the audiences to understand and observe mechanisms of the smallest and biggest building blocks of life. This event was simulcast in 50 universities world.

Vimeo   **Official**

▶ The Listening Post

by Frame

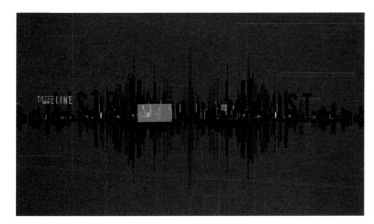 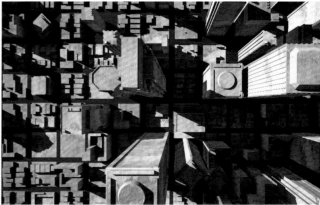

Creative Direction
Frame

Executive Production
Thomas Bay

**Motion Direction,
Animation & Composition**
Tom Crate

Design
Sebastian Onufszak

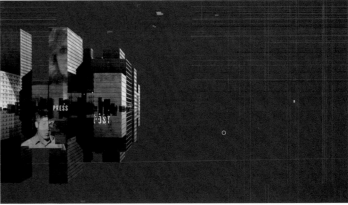

The media landscape is constantly changing. As platforms merge and diverge the message becomes fractured.

The Listening Post navigates a path, revealing what lies behind the story. It aims to monitor all forms of media, from network to bloggers, and report on what they do or dot not cover. It is the source of the ultimate truth: the blueprint of the media metropolis. It shows the background story of each headline and its political and economic connections.

The promo starts with an audio waveform, which transforms into a cityscape of buildings, representing the different media and their messages.

Vimeo **Official**

▶ ED AWARDS

by Tony Zagoraios

3D Supervision
Costas Fatsis

**3D Modelling, Lighting &
Texturing**
Stavros Karagiannis,
Orestis Aleksiewicz,
Angelos Roditakis

**Character Rigging &
Modelling**
Angelos Roditakis

FX Art
George Papaioanou

Composition
Rousselos Aravantinos

Graphic Design
Chris Golfis

Additional 2D Animation
Giorgos Eleftheroglou

Music Composition
Ted Regklis

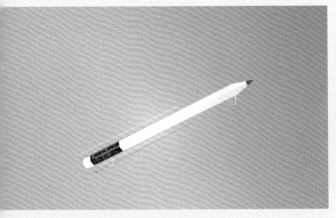

Tony Zagoraios and his team were invited to create the teaser for the European Design Awards 2015. Mainly inspired by the black and white colours of the updated logo, the design team decided to create a poetic and lyric moving image. It is a visual representation of the magical journey that each creative person is following to make any idea happen.

Vimeo   **Official**

▶ DINA LYNNYK SS17

by Eugene Pylinsky

 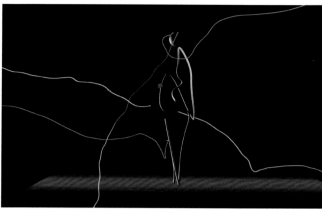

Music
Sommer

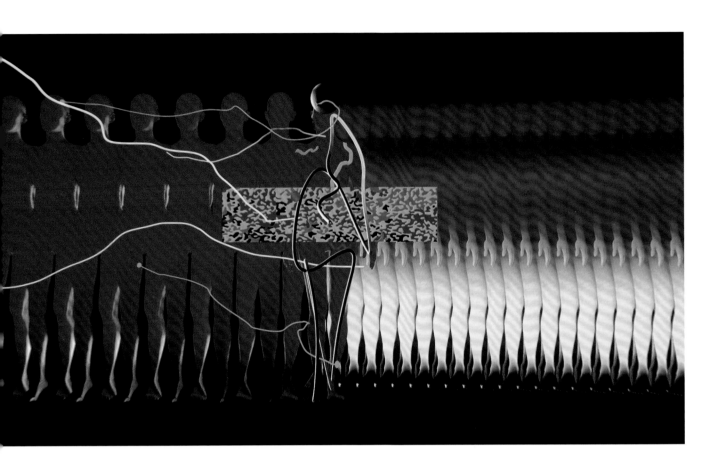

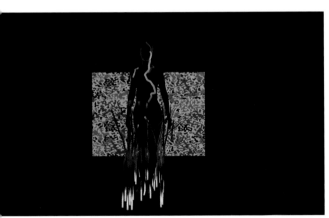

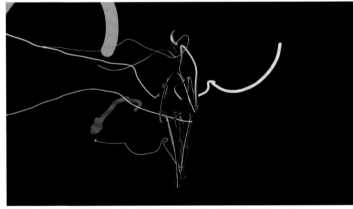

In collaboration with Dina Lynnyk, who is a Kyiv-based fashion designer, Eugene Pylinsky made three different videos — invitation, teaser, and catwalk intro. He used colours and shapes to create a surreal world which fit with the designer's collection and moodboard.

Vimeo   **Official**

▶ Resistance

by Eugene Pylinsky

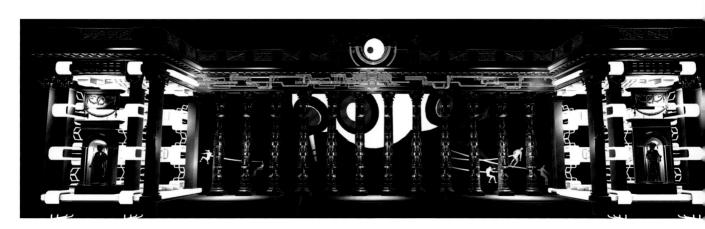

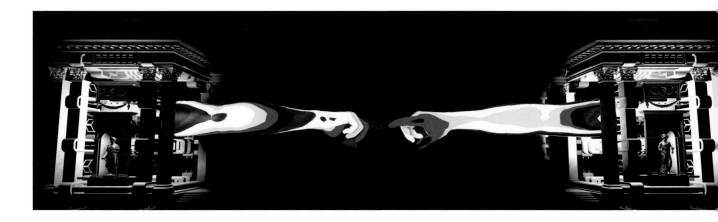

Music
Sunchase (aka. Alexander Pavlenko)

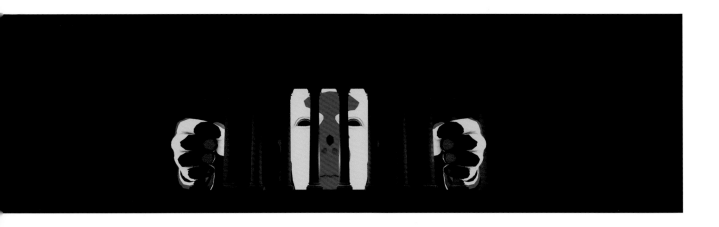

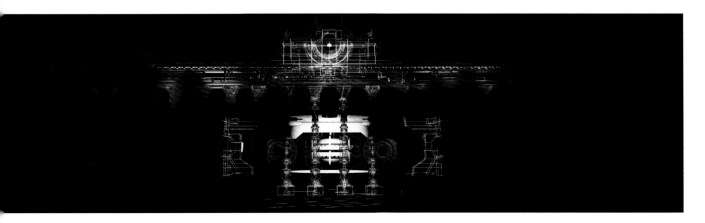

Inspired by animated short films Animatrix, this real-time
3D projection mapping was made for the Ukrainian Odessa
Light Festival.

Vimeo   **Official**

▶ Philip Larkin — High Windows

by Troublemakers

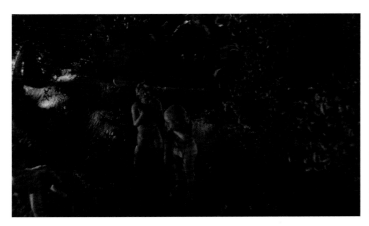
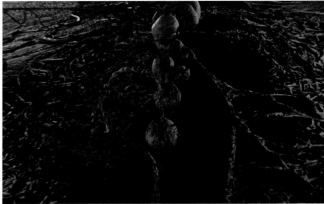

Director at JHP Foundation
Eleanor Carter

Creative Director Poetry Film Project
John-Paul Pryor

Direction
Onur Senturk

Production Company
Troublemakers

Production
James Hagger

Production Assistant
Felipe Bernard

Sculpture
Onur Senturk, Omer Kasimoglu

Title Design
Ipek Torun

Sound Design & Music
Cypheraudio

Cello
Michael Olsen

Sound Design, Production & Mix
John Black

Voice Over
Harold Pinter

Client
Josephine Hart
Poetry Foundation

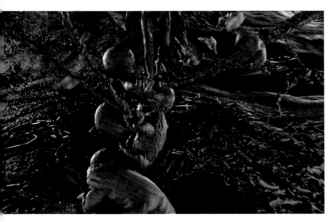

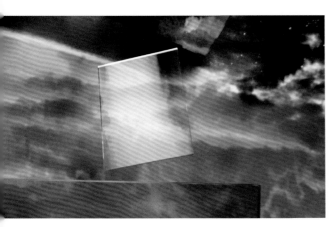
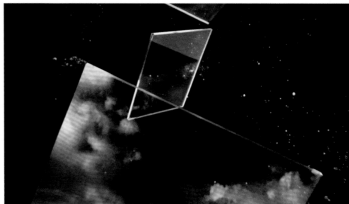

A POEM BY PHILIP LARKIN
HIGH WINDOWS

This animation is based on the poem "High Windows" by Philip Larkin, and one of the three films created for the launch of the Poetry Movement. Directed by Onur Senturk, the film explores the eternal themes of life and death. The Josephine Hart Poetry Foundation was set up by Lord Saatchi to further the advancement of arts, culture, and education, with a focus on poetry, literature, and dynamitic performance.

Vimeo   **Official**

▶ T.S. Eliot — The Wasteland

by Troublemakers

Director of the JHP Foundation
Eleanor Carter

Creative Director Poetry Film Project
John-Paul Pryor

Production Company
Troublemakers

Direction
Icecream

Production
James Hagger

Production Assistant
Felipe Bernard

Additional Animation
Simon Lebon

Sound Design & Music
Cypheraudio

Sound Design, Production & Mix
John Black

Voice Over
Robert Montgomery

Client
Josephine Hart Foundation

This video is one of the three films created for the launch of the Poetry Movement, which was initiated by The Josephine Hart Poetry Foundation. Through this movement, they want to stand as the next logical step in terms of the way people consume verse. It will grow and develop into a creative space that encapsulates the beauty of imagination and inventiveness.

"T S Eliot — The Wasteland" is based on T.S. Eliot's "The Wasteland." Directed by Icecream (aka Nico Dufoure), the film is set in a post-apocalyptic virus-stricken world to illustrate the disillusionment of a generation and a separation from belief.

Vimeo **Official**

▶ TRANS H. Spectrum Conf 2016
by Whitelight Motion

**Curating &
Key Visual Design**
OzzieArt

Creative Agency
Whitelight Motion

**Direction &
Motion Supervision**
Rex Hon

CG Art
Children Chiu

2D Motion Design
Bruce Chen

Grading
Rex Hon

Composition
Rex Hon

Sound Design
Wen-Hsimg Wang

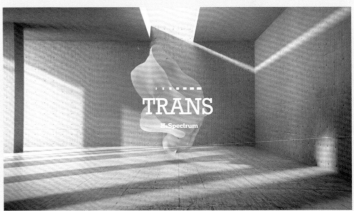

TRANS, H. Spectrum provides a platform for healthcare start-ups' founders, investors, students, and professionals to meet and connect.

It is H. Spectrum's vision that boost the trend of healthcare start-ups and to groom the entrepreneur community in Taiwan. Since the prevailing mindset is based on the concept of scaling existing business models from 1 to N, H. Spectrum tried to seed the concepts of zero to one, and thinking outside the box to facilitate creativity and innovation.

Vimeo   **Official**

▶ World Hockey Championship Opening St.Petersburg 2016

by Radugadesign

Production
Aleksei Lozhkin, Irina S fiullina,
Ksusha Chekhovskaya

Art Direction
Nikolay Kulyakhtin

Modelling
Yuriy Snitko, Roman Chumak

3D Art
Artur Zhamaletdinov,
Dmitriy Kulikov

Sound FX
Veniamin Raev

Radugadesign participated in the opening ceremony of the World Hockey Championship in two cities simultaneously — Moscow and St. Petersburg. Both shows were devoted to this grand event, but they were different in their content. They introduce the material prepared for the ceremony in Saint Petersburg. Every match of the tournament started with this video.

Vimeo   Official

▶ Tipooo Opening

by Felipe Frazão

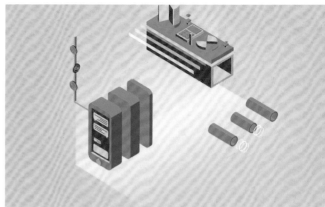

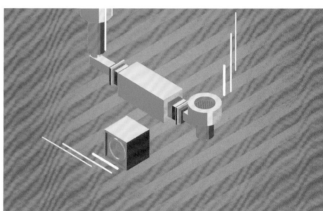
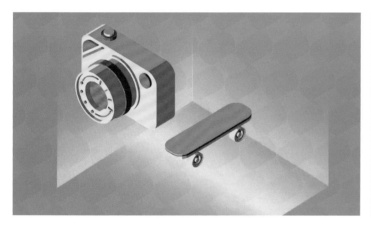

Creative Direction
Fábio Acorsi

Design & Main Animation
Felipe Frazão

Additional Animation
Cauê Mendes

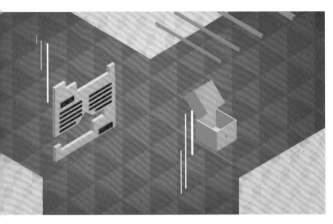
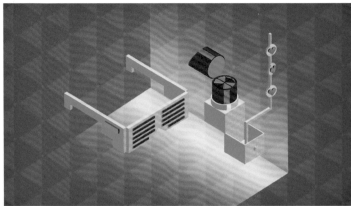
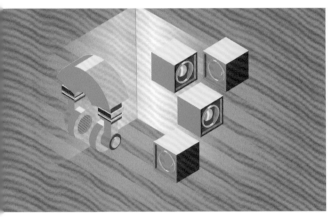
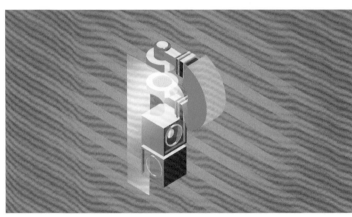
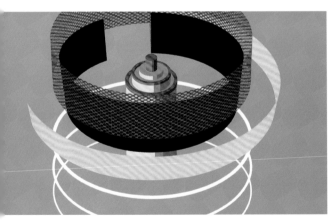

This film was designed and animated for the opening of a Brazilian teen program project called Tipooo in the year 2015.

Set in a sheer colour background, the narrative begins with a block dynamically transforming into various objects that pile up to be different characters and form the project name orderly. The eye-catching colour palette generates an energetic picture and invokes a sense of youth, power, and vitality.

Vimeo

▶ Call of Duty — Interactive Trailers

by Jonathan Kim

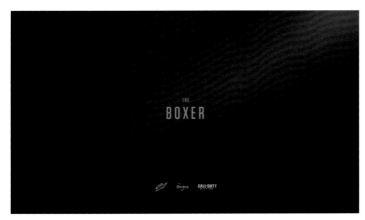 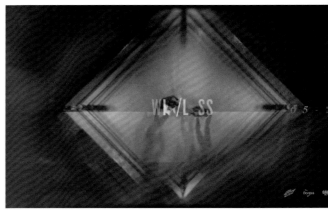

Production
Firstborn

Creative Direction & Design
Jonathan Kim

Design
Rachael Park, Yun Chen

Composition
Bruno Ferrari, Yun Chen

Animation
Michael Kuzmich,
Bruno Ferrari, Rachael Park,
Erica Hu, Yun Chen

3D Design
Ron White, Jay Harwood

3D Character Animation
Mike Bourbeau

Copy
Sam Isenstein

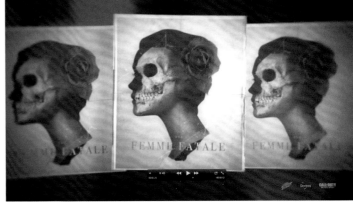

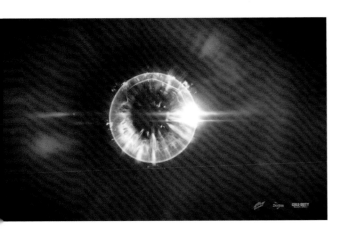

This film is composed of three cinematic trailers with an interactive twist. Viewers used the camera on their computers to take a photo of themselves and watch as they become a cast member within the trailers, in real time.

Vimeo   **Official**

▶ Lar Center

by Felipe Frazão

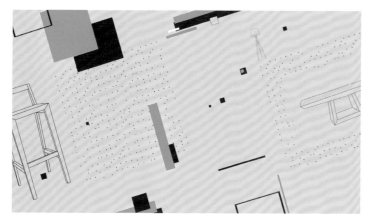 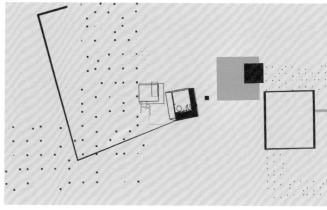

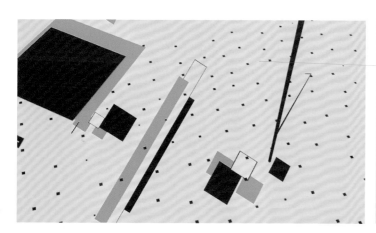 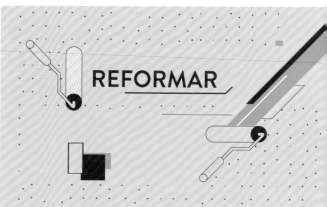

**Art Direction,
Design & Animation**
Felipe Frazão

Direction
Mateus de Paula

Animation
Fabiano Broki

Vetor Zero
Lobo

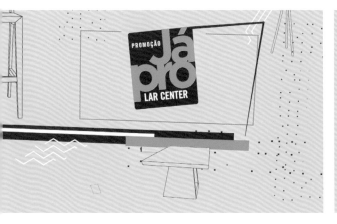

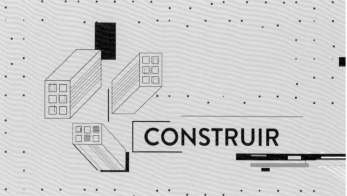

This film was created for a promotion campaign initiated by
Lar Center, which is a shopping mall in Brazil.

Vimeo

▶ **A Call to Say Hello — BAYA (OBSCENIC Records)**

by John Christian Ferner Apalnes

Direction & Photography
Andreas Bjørseth

Animation
John Christian Ferner Apalnes

John Christian Ferner Apalnes was invited to animate this video to give the storytelling an additional layer. This Music Video and Documentary deals with Baya's quest to find his roots and identity. He enhances the complexities related to Baya's quest by animation, through overlaying footage with contrasting animation and narrative allusions.

Vimeo

▶ Chai

by Daniel Moreno Cordero

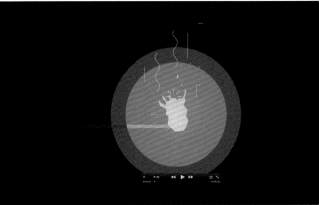

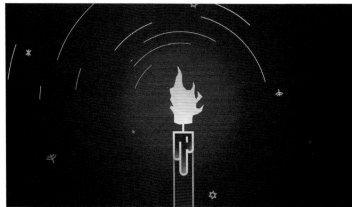

Daniel Moreno Cordero made the design and animation for this fun project, explaining some parts of the Jewish culture, for the IFCJ organization.

Chai means "Life" in Hebrew, and since every Hebrew alphabet has a value, Chai equals 18, which is a very important number for the Hebrew. It is often seen in the toasting, such as "Chai to Life." This film makes the word feel more alive, refreshing, and fun.

Vimeo   **Official**

▶ MineShine Yearbook
by MixCode

Agency
Bremen

Direction
MixCode

Art
TuBo Lee, HuiYing Kao

2D Animation
Chiunyi.ko, HuiYing Kao,
Ching Huang, Mibo Lin,
Hank Chen, Kyle Jhuang

3D Animation
Chiunyi.ko, Shih Yao Chang

Music & Sound Design
Pongo

Client
Uni-President

This is a montage of a series of animated clips for an interactive website event named MineShine Yearbook. The young who is going to graduate from school can send a delicately animated film with lovely messages to their friends by the website. Each film is consisted of three short clips. All the clips are energetic and colourful, like their youth.

Vimeo   **Official**

▶ Ladi6 — Beffy

by Parallel Teeth

Music
Ladi6

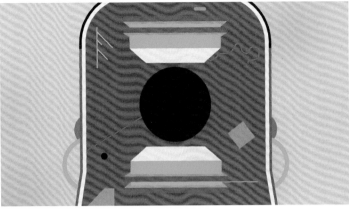

This animated music video tells a tale of friendship and unity. The visuals rhythmically unfold around the song, carefully replicating the audio's twists and turns. Bright colours, geometric shapes and unrealistic perspectives are used to create the lively world.

Vimeo   **Official**

► Eliminatorias TyC Sports

by Lumbre

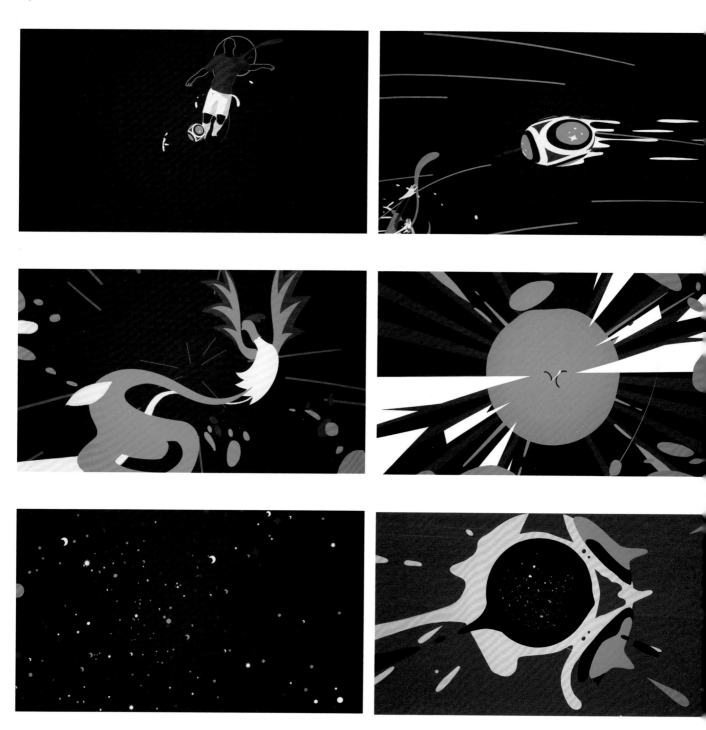

Client
TyC Sports

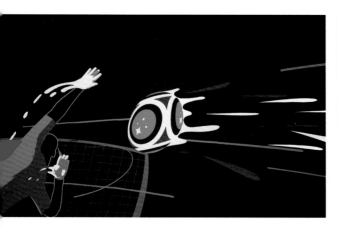
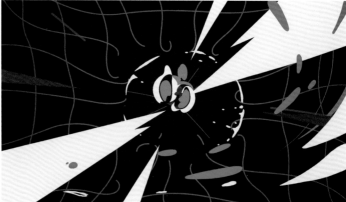
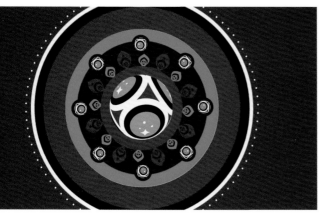

One of a Program Packaging for elimination rounds for the
2018 FIA World Cup in Russia.

Vimeo   Official

▶ Merk — I'm Easy

by Parallel Teeth

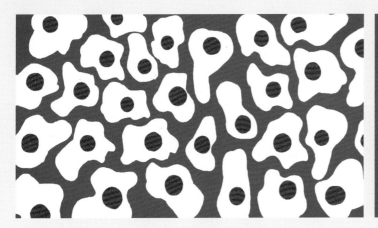

Music
Merk

**Illustration,
Animation & Rotoscoping**
Parallel Teeth,
Caitlin McCarthy

Live Action Camera Op
Josh Yong

Parallel Teeth made this playfully animated music video for Merk's vibrant track "I'm Easy" featuring a cast of whimsical characters. The clip wasn't created with a strict storyboard, instead the video's narrative evolved organically as the animation was created. Throughout the project, the keywords for the project were bold, loose and playful.

Vimeo   **Official**

▶ 2015 Vivid Sydney — Sydney Opera House "Lighting the Sails"

by MixCode

Creative Direction
Matt: Pyke – Universal
Everything

Production
Greg Povey

Direction & Art
MixCode

Animation
Chiunyi Ko, TuBo Lee,
Paz Lee, Mibo Lin, Cathy Ho,
Roy Hsia, Ching, Zi Qian Liu

Sound Design
Sincerely Music Simon
Pyke – Freefarm

Client
Sydney Opera House

The Cel animation is part of the Vivid 2015: Lighting the Sails project, a projection mapped onto Sydney Opera House during the middle of 2015. The keyword is "Attack." It starts with a man breaking the chains, then transforms into growling animals, and ends with the hand gesture of a dove to indicate their core value: anti-war.

Vimeo   **Official**

▶ Starry Night

by Cobb Studio

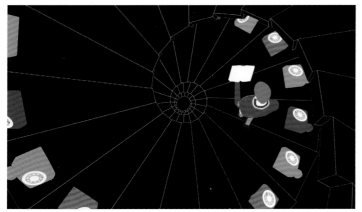
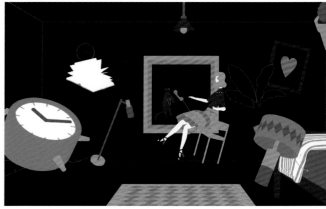

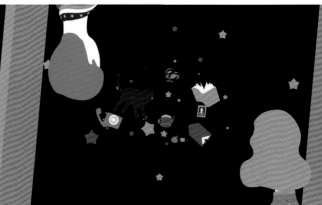

Direction
Shinyoung Kim

Production
Wonseok Lee

Artwork
Shinyoung Kim

Starry Night is a music video for Shinee Onew and Lee Jinah. The story is about a girl and a boy who miss each other every night as they stare at the stars in the sky. But because of their distance, their daily lives seem slow and repetitive, and stars pile up as their longing becomes intense. The repetitive patterns and scenes appearing and reappearing in this video emphasise such feeling, highlighted by surreal and stylish artwork by Shinyoung Kim.

Vimeo **Official**

▶ GATE 212 — Give Me That Dive

by John Christian Ferner Apalnes

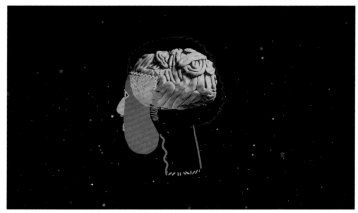
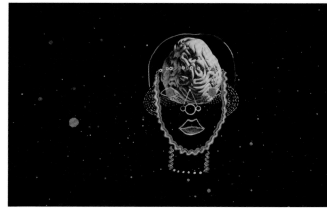
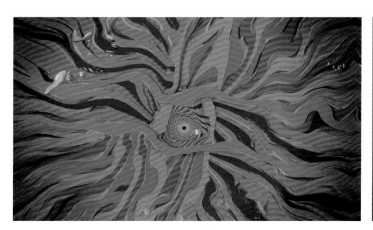
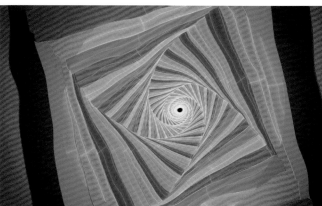

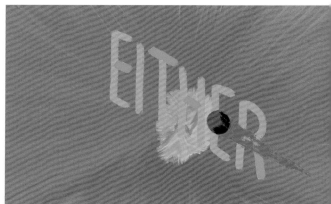

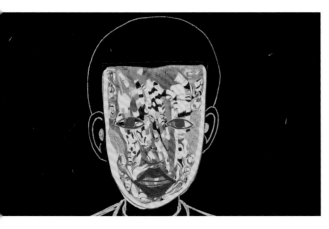

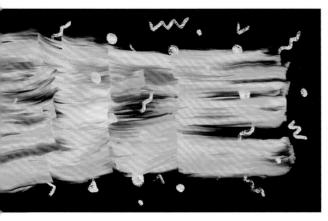
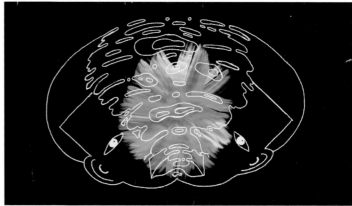
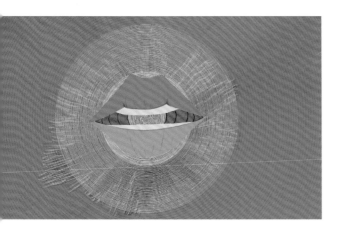

This video was made to accompany Baya's live performance. Baya's music and ideology are highly informed by the duality and transformation the musician himself has gone through. So it was crucial to capture a sense of duplexity and constant movement in the visuals. He plays with different techniques and colourful contrasts to pull the viewer into this world. John Christian Ferner Apalnes used stra-to-cut, stop-motion, and 2D-cel animation to populate this universe.

Vimeo   Official

► Angels / Your Love

by John Christian Ferner Apalnes

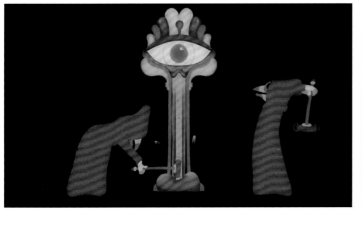 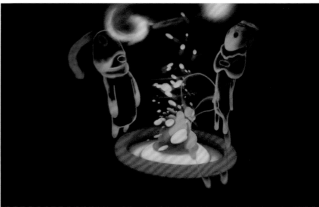

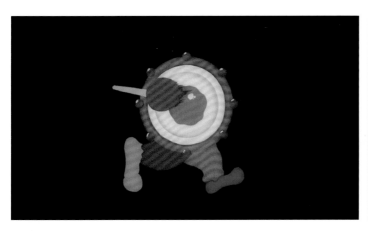 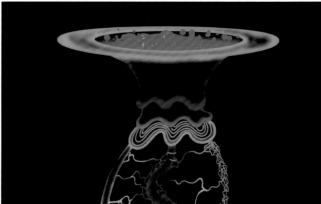

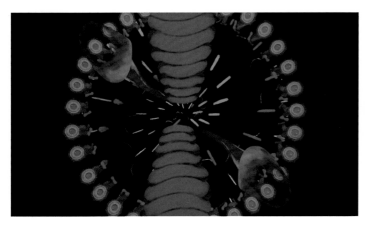 

Production
Strange Beast

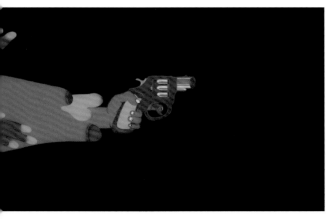
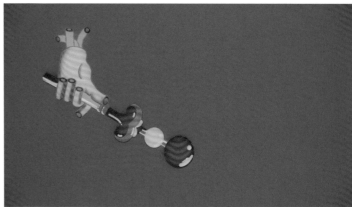

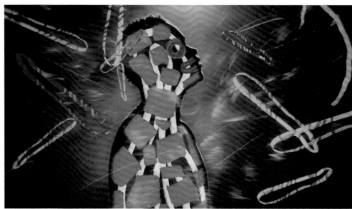

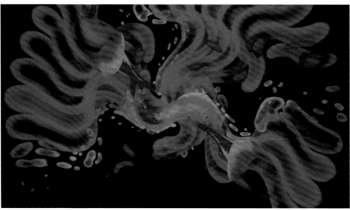

John Christian Ferner Apalnes wanted to capture the joy and exuberance of the collaboration between Jack and BJ The Chicago Kid, by building a strange world bursting with colours and fizzing with energetic transformations to emphasise the direction in the song.

The finished video pulls together bright, ghostly animation and footage of BJ in a surreal combination that twists and turns with the song. Pushing the boundaries of what could be achieved, he used a mashup of techniques with frame by frame animation, rotoscoping, live action, and 3D elements, all interacting together.

Youtube   **Official**

▶ 51st Montreux Jazz Festival

by nöbl.tv

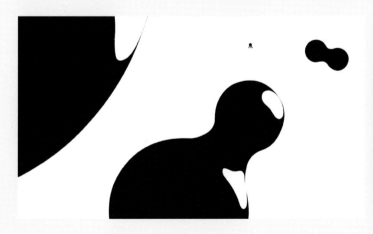

Direction
nöbl

Design
Jonathan Djob Nkondo

Production
Messieurs.ch

Animation
Jonathan Djob Nkondo,
Wen Fan, nöbl

Musique
The good lie by Warhaus

Client
Montreux Jazz Festival

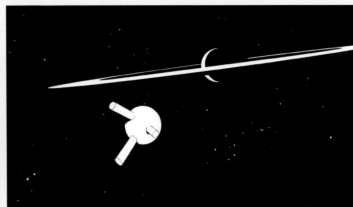
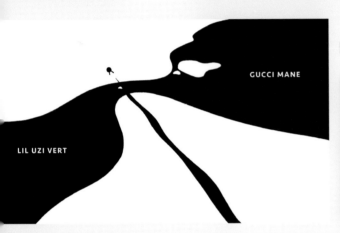

This trailer was created to announce lineup artists of
Montreux Jazz festival 2017.

Vimeo   **Official**

▶ Pause Fest — Overrated Reality

by Sociedad Fantasma

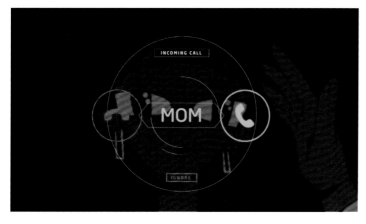

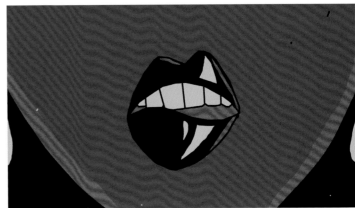

Pause Festival invited Sociedad Fantasma to participate in the Motion Response Challenge based on the Festival's annual theme: Different Perspective. Sociedad Fantasma created a time where reality is overrated.

Vimeo   Official

▶ Fashion Business School at London College of Fashion

by Territory Studio

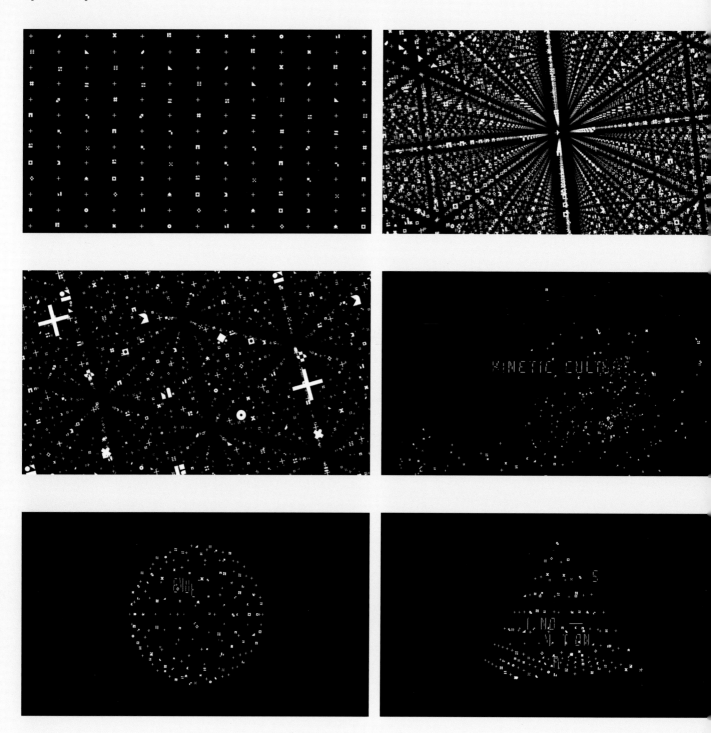

Client
Alphabetical Studio

Note
British Design and
Art Direction (D&AD) Winner

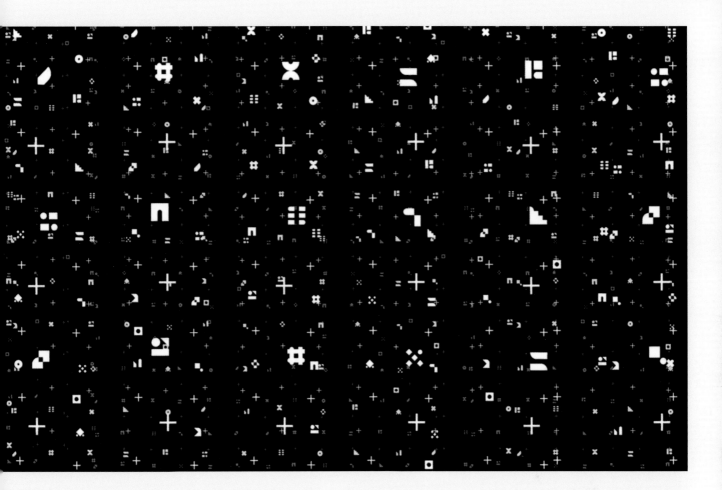

Briefed to create a series of dynamic animations for the launch event of Fashion Business School at London College of Fashion, Territory crafted a stunning graphic interpretation of excellence, innovation and breadth of vision. Informed by a set of bespoke icons inspired by pattern cutting design and representative of key themes, Territory devised five narrative concepts to bring each one to life on screen. Beautifully choreographed to an original sound track, the icons transform from static symbols suspended on a strict grid to free flowing organic forms — their dynamic transformation is a poignant reference to the creative craft of fashion itself.

Vimeo   **Official**

▶ The Design Mine — The Future of Fabric Design

by Jiaqi Wang

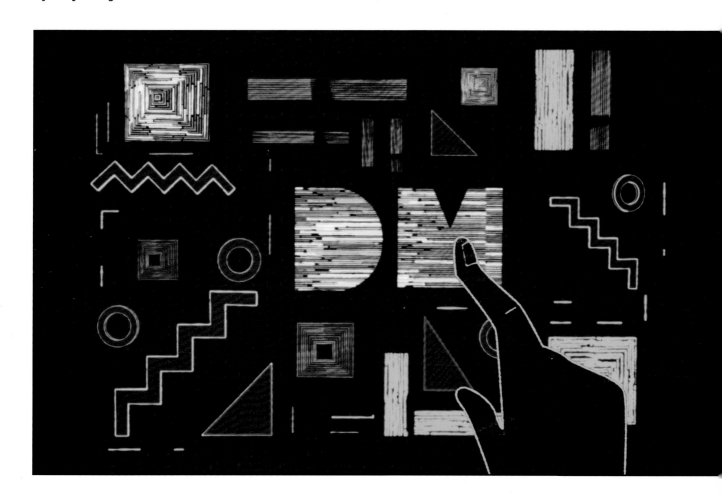

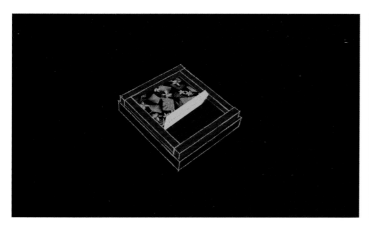

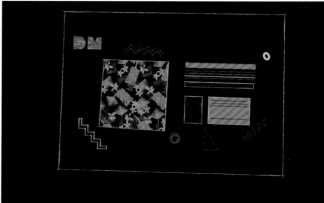

Art Direction
The Design Mine

Music
Bea Munro

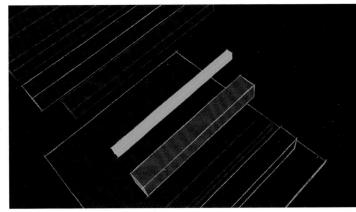
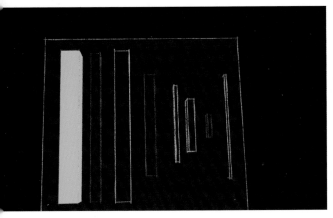
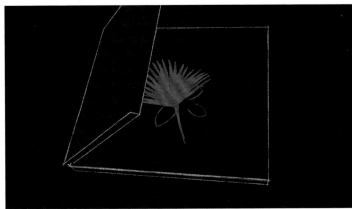

The Design Mine is an innovative textile marketplace connecting designers with buyers, providing trend insight and delivering digital textile files. Designers can showcase and sell their work so that buyers can bring their collections to life. Their sustainable solutions enable them to be the future of fabric design.

Vimeo   **Official**

▶ Can Factory

by Jhao-Yu Shih

In an imaginary forest, every seed will be baptized by a fantastic factory to become part of the forest. There is a curious and optimistic seed, which also gets into the factory with other seeds, looking forward to become part of the forest. However, it later finds it absurd to become the same with the other seeds, and strives to be a unique one. Jhao-Yu Shih illustrated and directed this film, embodying this story with an innocent and fantastic aura for a serious topic. It delves into our deep memory of our parent's expectations, social rules, and moral limitations that have been imposed on us since our childhood. Jhao-Yu consequently rethinks this memory using a fairy-like manner.

Youtube   **Official**

▶ Senna, in the heart of Brazil

by Le Cube

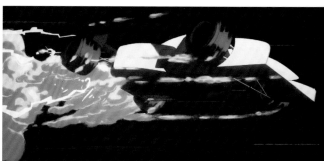

▶ Senna, in the heart of Brazil

by Le Cube

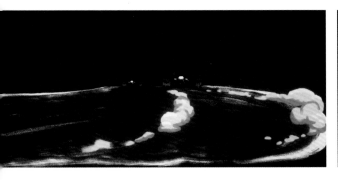
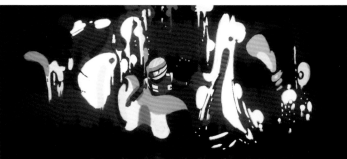

Senna is more than a Formula 1 racer; for Brazilians, he is a hero, an icon of overcoming hardship, stubbornness and good character. For the 2016 Olympic Games in Rio de Janeiro, together with JWT and "Instituto Ayrton Senna," an NGO by Senna's family, Le Cube has prepared a beautiful message from Senna to all the Brazilian Olympic athletes, pointing out the importance of winning at home. Ayrton Senna lost eight times before winning the Brazilian GP, and when he did, it was with a lot of effort. Still he faced it unflinchingly.

Vimeo   Official

▶ Parrot Kitchen Open

by INLAND STUDIO

Design Agency
Daydreamer

**Creative Direction &
Art Direction**
INLAND STUDIO

Illustration
Cynthia Alonso

Animation
Matias Sesti (INLAND STUDIO)

INLAND STUDIO was commissioned to produce a new graphic
pack for a Chinese cooking show "Kitchen Parrot." They seek
to evoke the tradition and history by using an artistically
strong style that brings to life a colourful and cool art.

Vimeo   **Official**

▶ Sentirte Bien

by INLAND STUDIO

Casa Club TV reached out to INLAND STUDIO to develop a graphic pack of "Sentirte Bien" series. In this project, INLAND STUDIO worked under the concept "lifestyle in harmony," designing a world where nature comes to life and invites people to approach it in a friendly manner.

Vimeo

Official

▶ Voice of Figures

by Radugadesign

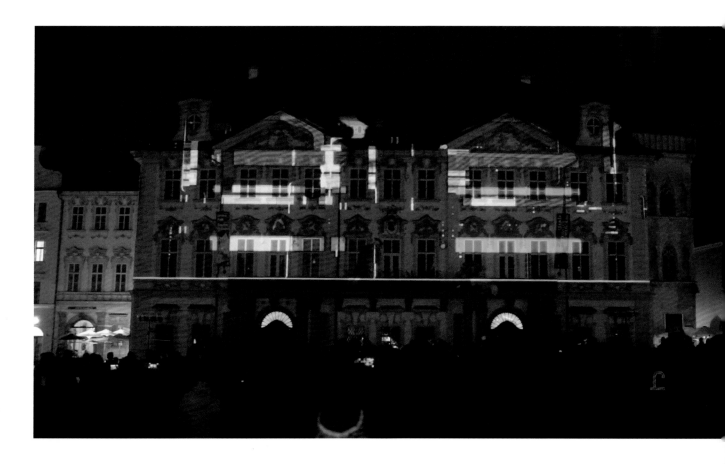

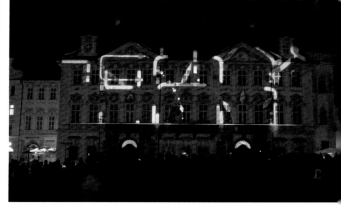

Creative Production
Ksusha Chekhovskaya

Media Art
Artemy Perevertin

Music
Alexander Zaripov

Creative Direction
Ivan Nefedkin, Mikhail Kabatov

Film Direction
Alexey Ustinov

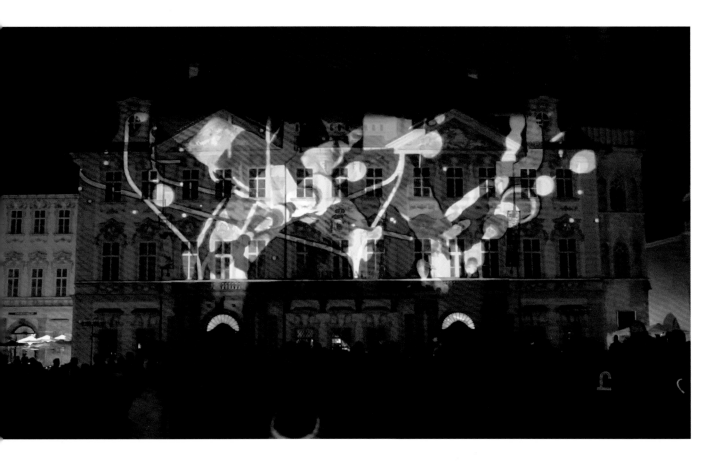

Radugadesign created this bright and positive work called "Voice of Figures," which opened the festival at the Old Town Square in the heart of Prague. The installation consists of a projection for the facade of the National Gallery, where they have used an original approach in terms of architectural mapping. The concept of audio-visual installation and the major generator for graphics was the music composed by the young composer Alexander Zaripov. Installation did not follow the rules of 3D mapping, where the correct picture can only be disclosed in terms of the "ideal spectator." Thanks to this concept, "Voice of Figures" was well-viewed from different points of large and populous area. The feature of the work was universality. The graphics, as with any projection for a facade, subject to architectural forms, but it was not too difficult to scale and adapt it for another surface, interior, more complex pattern or a straight wall.

Vimeo   **Official**

...BUM COVER

...CISED BABY SHOWS
UNDERWATER BOY,
A US DOLLAR BILL ON A FISHHOOK
JUST OUT OF HIS REACH.
...ED THE IDEA WHILE WATCHING
WATER BIRTHS WITH GROHL. COBAIN
...FEN'S ART DIRECTOR ROBERT FISHER.
SOME STOCK FOOTAGE OF UNDERWATER
BIRTHS BUT THEY WERE TOO GRAPHIC
FOR THE RECORD COMPANY. ALSO, THE STOCK
HOUSE THAT CONTROLLED THE PHOTO OF
A SWIMMING BABY THAT THEY SUBSEQUENTLY
SETTLED ON WANTED $7,500 A YEAR FOR
ITS USE, SO INSTEAD FISHER SENT A PHOTOGRAPHER
TO A POOL FOR BABIES TO TAKE PICTURES.
FIVE SHOTS RESULTED AND THE BAND SETTLED
ON THE IMAGE OF A THREE-MONTH-OLD INFANT NAMED
SPENCER ELDEN, THE SON OF THE PHOTOGRAPHER'S
THERE WAS ...THE CONCERN BECAUSE ELDEN'S CIRCUMCISED
...BLE IN THE IMAGE. GEFFEN PREPARED AN ALTERNATE
THE PENIS, ...THEY WERE AFRAID THAT IT WOULD
...PLE, BUT ...PRESENTED WHEN COBAIN MADE IT CLEAR THAT
...MISE HE WOULD ACCEPT WAS A STICKER COVERING
...SAY, "IF YOU'RE
YOU ... BE A CLOSET PEDOPHILE"
WOULD

BUT IF NOT...
JUMP IN, BABY

NEVERMIND

1/60day

Type

▶ Skolkovo

by Loop

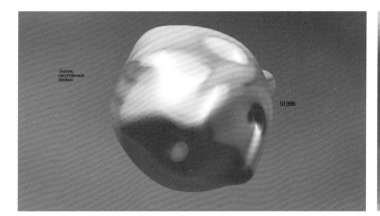
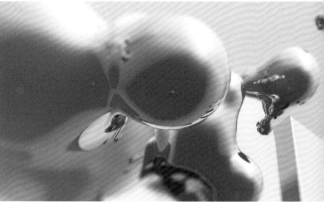

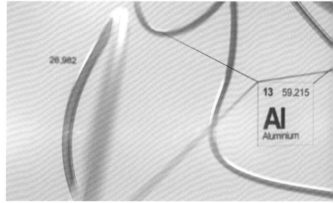

Agency
MIR

Art Direction
Alex Mikhaylov

Design
Alex Mikhaylov

Animation
Alex Mikhaylov, Danil Peshkov,
Pavel Skalkin, Roman Senko

Rendering
Alex Mikhaylov,
Max Chelyadnikov,
Pavel Skalkin

Composition
Alex Mikhaylov

Client
Skolkovo

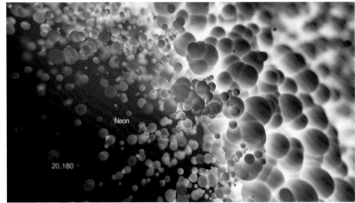

Skolkovo is the largest Innovation and Research Centre based in Russia. This film is a commercial spot to publishing the institution. In order to show its scientific background, the designers used varied elements to convey the concept, including liquid, crystallization, atom, metal, and DNA sequences.

Vimeo   **Official**

▶ Northwestern Mutual — Event Film

by Jonathan Kim

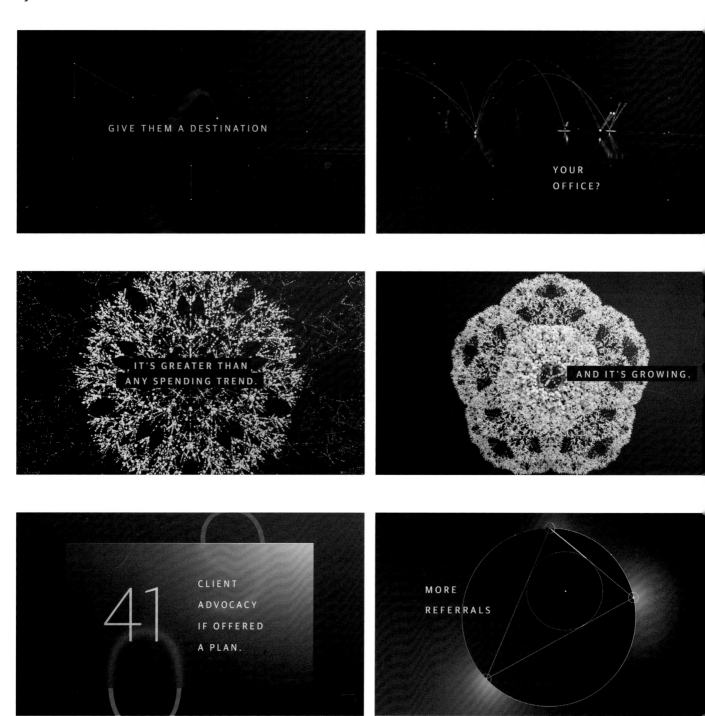

Design Agency
Rare Volume

LARGER THAN
THE SUM OF EVERY
LINKED ACCOUNT.

MORE THAN

25K

PREMIUM PAYMENTS
EVERY MONTH.

FINANCIAL
REPRESENTATIVES
WHO PLAN HAVE

2X

THE SALES DOLLARS
IN YEAR ONE.

THEIR
OFFICE?

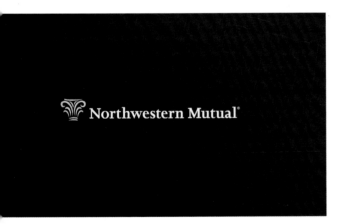

Northwestern Mutual®

A fun and energetic infographics film used to educate Northwestern Mutual employees on the power of the new and improved northwesternmutual.com.

Vimeo

▶ Genesis

by Panoply

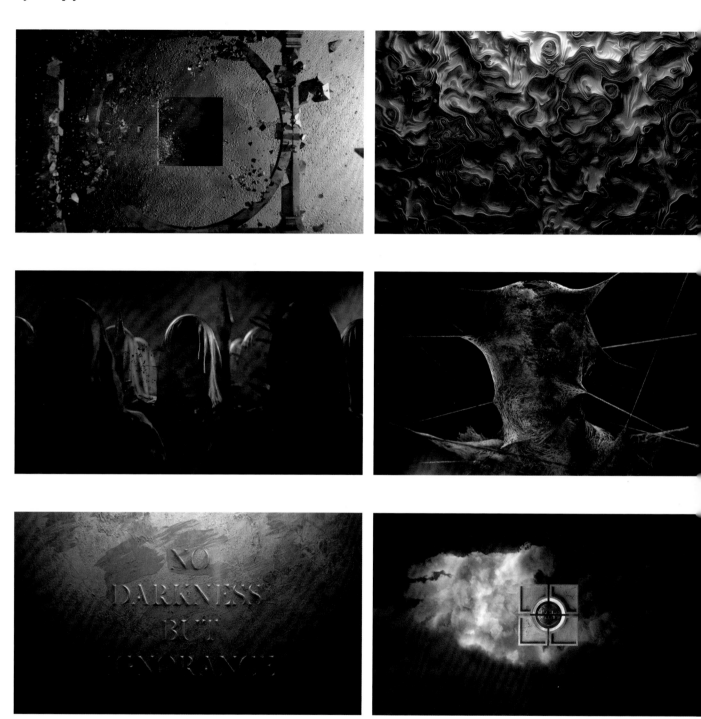

Creative Direction
Renaud Futterer, Mark Lindner

Audio
Echoic Audio

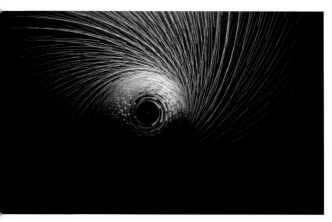

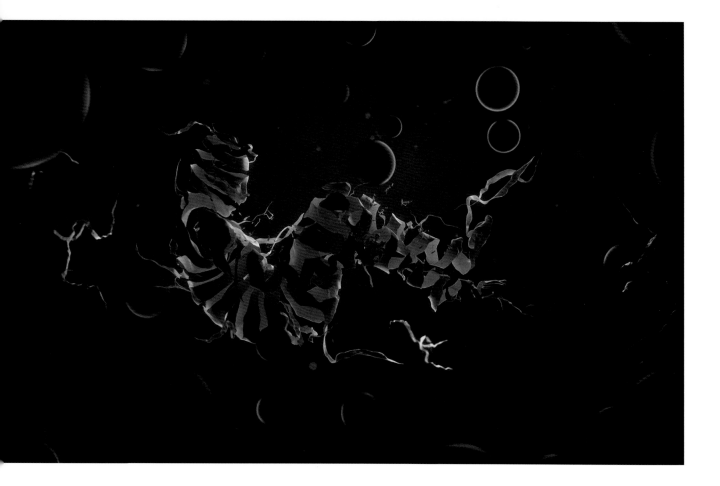

Through a combination of powerful imagery and atmospheric pace Genesis dares the audiences to fleetingly glimpse their own origins, their civilisation, and the known universe.

Drawing heavily on a visual currency distilled from the subconscious and the psychology of self, the film is taken on a stark journey marrying rippling, organic forms with stern, unyielding geometry. Inspiration for Genesis was predominantly drawn from Carl Jung's writing, in particular his last work *Man and His Symbols*. Consequently, the designers were instantly engaged by the myriad of reoccurring signs and symbols that have historically been replicated by seemingly unrelated cultures and societies. This phenomenon alludes to a vast, collective visual language that stems from the human subconscious, shaped by the world.

Vimeo   **Official**

▶ Gravity

by Clemens Wirth

Direction
Clemens Wirth

Music & Sound
Radium Audio

Clemens Wirth created this eye-catching experimental short film. Analogue experiments with gravity set to a pulsating instrumental score.

In this project, he designed a control panel, which can be rotated 360° to determine the direction, and a horizontal measurement to define the strength at the bottom. Upon this setting, he experiments with different materials, all of which are made of physical effect, based on the laws of gravity.

Vimeo   **Official**

▶ Pause 2016 Motion Response — Discovery

by Ranger & Fox

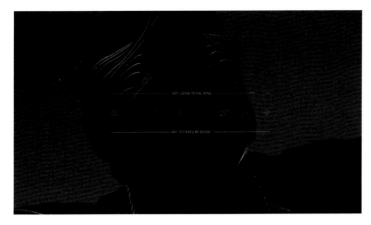 

 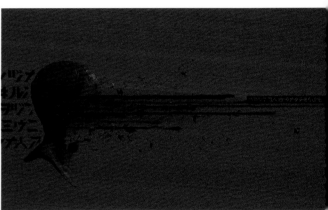

Direction
Brett Morris, Steve Panicara

Model Design
Patrick Goski

Music
Zelig Sound

Note
AGDA Distinction in
Motion 2016

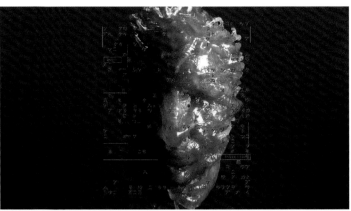

Pause is Australia's premier Creative, Tech and Business event empowering creators since 2011.

For their 2016 motion response, Brett Morris and Steve Panicara considered that people are often faced with so many decisions — decisions that can have little effect or be so monumental that they can be life altering. Uncertainty and restraint hold us back while boldness can push us to places where we never thought possible. Ideas are challenged, adversity will be faced and the end result not always predictable. Discovering your future self is a journey all about finding the beauty on that unpredictable path.

They finally achieve a look that is almost abstract and philosophical with the head statue decomposing, melting, rotating, and cracking, showing that change is always suffused with self-question and self-deconstruction. Paralleled with Kenji Miyazawa's poem, the film leads up to a breath-taking piece.

Vimeo   **Official**

▶ Fox Sports — World Cup 2014 GFX

by 4HUMANS

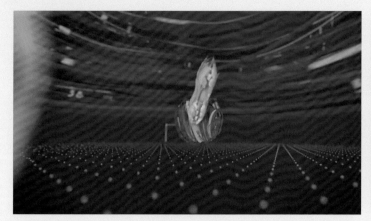

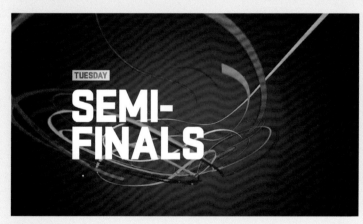

Direction
Facu Labo

Development
Josefina Llano

Client
Fox Latinamerica

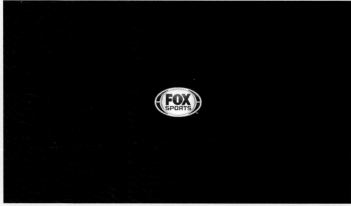

Fox Sports commissioned 4HUMANS to develop the overall visual impression for all of their channels in Latin America for the World Cup 2014. The 4HUMANS in-house team finished the task amazingly by creating and animating the package.

The fundamental colour palette is composed of green and blue which reminds audience of the Brazilian national flag. The colourful filiform stadiums and renowned landmarks, paired with cheerful music, showcase the charm of Brazil and generate a carnival atmosphere for the passionate football fans from all over the world.

Vimeo   **Official**

▶ MTV EMA16 — Promo Toolkit

by INLAND STUDIO

Production Company INLAND STUDIO	**Motion Graphics** Julian Nuñez, Gonzalo Nogues	**Designer Lead** Charlx Alemañy	**Production Management** Delfina Chiesa
Art Direction Gonzalo Nogues	**VP Creative** Sean Saylor	**Motion Design** Federico Maksimiuk	**Production** Camila González
Design Javier Bernales, Gonzalo Nogues	**Creative Direction** Maxi Borrego	**Director Production &** **Operation** Josefina Marfil	**Client** MTV World Creative Studio

MTV World Creative Studio approached INLAND STUDIO to produce the promotional material for EMA 2016, the MTV's year event. They challenged INLAND STUDIO to create an editable but complex system playing with images and an irreverent message in an independent system.

Vimeo   Official

▶ TOYOTA WISH MONOTONE
by Alld. inc.

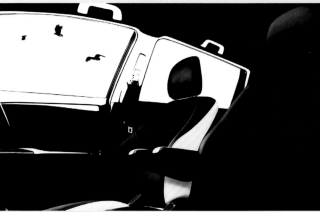

Art Direction
Kenichi Ogino (ALLd. inc.)

Motion Design
Masakazu Nomura

Design
Fumiya Hirose (ALLd. inc.)

Production
Gyosei Okada (PUZZLE)

© TOYOTA

The TV commercial video was designed for the debut of two new black and white specially equipped cars of Toyota — TOYOTA WISH MONOTONE.

The aesthetic abstract world was realized by the contrast of "black" and "white." In this motion graphic, the contrast of "stillness" and "motion" was drawn to emphasize existence as well. The scenes are very minimalistic, filled with common driving scenes and sometimes Japanese painting alike natural elements. Alongside with cosy music, the final result depicts a romantic and adventurous journey that Toyata invites their users to explore with the two cars.

Vimeo   **Official**

▶ OMULA BEAUTY CREATES
by Alld. inc.

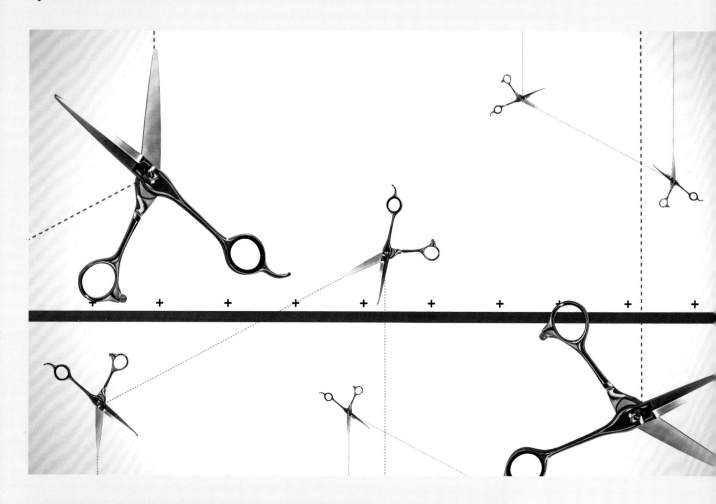

Creative Direction
Yashushi Kuroda (HAKUHODO)

Art Direction
Kenichi Ogino (ALLd. inc.)

Motion Design
Suguru Tachikawa,
Masakazu Nomura,
Takahiro Yamamichi

Design
Fumiya Hirose (ALLd. inc.),
Junko Fujie

Sound Design
Shuta Hasunuma,
Shinichiro Kobayakawa

Production
Norikazu Shimazaki
(Wonder Land House)

© OMULA BEAUTY CREATES

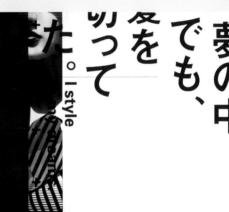

"OMULA BEAUTY CREATES" is a professional school for hair designers, makeup artists, and fashion designers. The motion graphic is a commercial movie for the brand.

In overview, it was created with synchronised typographic animation to music and used red as the main colour. Although the length of this film, comprised of 2 pieces in total, is merely 20 seconds, it conveys rich information, and leaves a long-lasting memory achieved by sophisticated layouts, exciting transitions, and elegant images and typography.

Vimeo **Official**

▶ One Data — TF1 Publicité

by nöbl.tv

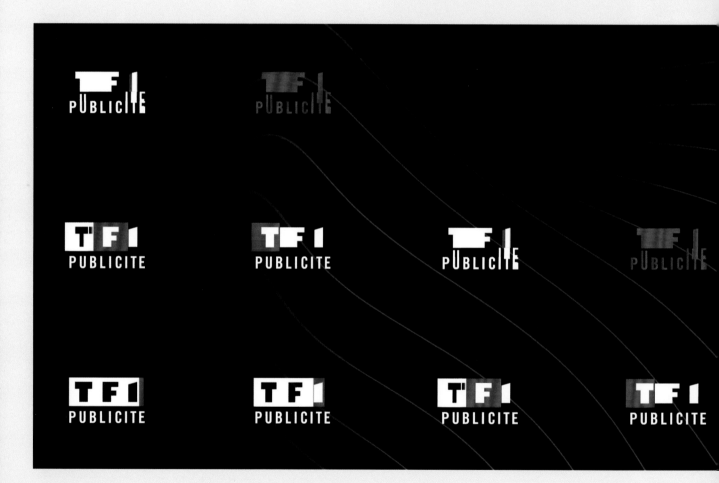

**Direction,
Design & Animation**
Julien Nantiec, Cyril Izarn

Graphic Identity
Montagnier Cyrille

Audio
Chut on vous écoute

Production
Tetro

Client
TF1 Publicité

The film was presented to the announcers of TF1 Publicité and to the press. One Data is an advertising offer of new generation, which combines the power of television and the traditional data with new forms of data. The graphic identity was revealed by a mechanical clip which is based on a division of the screen into nine parts, pop and dynamic, with a set of shifts and reversals.

Vimeo **Official**

▶ #Digitized14

by Alex Frukta

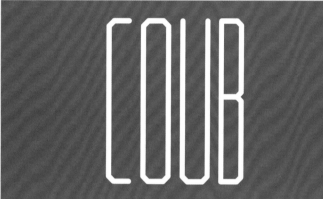
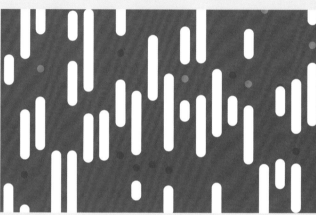

Concept,
Direction & Production
Nord Collective

Arseny Vesnin, the founder of Designcollector, was invited to speak at Digitized Conference in Athens to introduce top Russian independent start-ups that has been recognised across the globe, such as Glitche app, Anti-Selfie SLMMSK, COUB, Ready Mag, and Cirqle.

Nord Collective helped to make Opening titles for the presentation. Alex Frukta employed motifs and a constant colour palette of white and blue to introduce the brands, personalizing the logos through the fun animation.

Vimeo   **Official**

▶ Paris — New York

by Alex Frukta

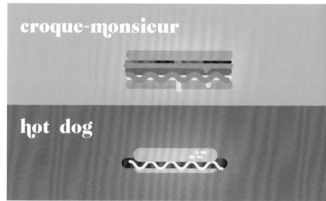

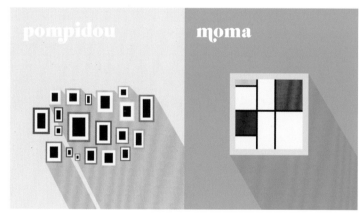

Design Agency
NORD Collective

Sound Design
The Cosmic Setter

In 2012 Penguin Books published Vahram Muratyan's book called "*Paris versus NewYork*." Being huge fans of Vahram's work, NORD Collective created the animated version of the book. To make this tribute real, the designers didn't use original illustrations directly, instead they used Vahram's ideas as base, completely reworked on the design and illustrations trying to keep visual similarity to original. Afterwards, they animated all scenes and invited The Cosmic Setter to write and perform original music and sound design for this project.

Vimeo **Official**

by Felipe Frazão

 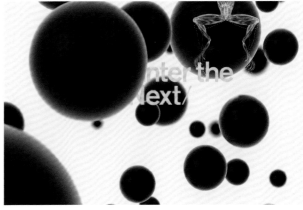

Agency
F/Nazca Saatchi & Saatchi

Production
LOBO

Creative Direction
Mateus de Paula

Modelling
(heart) Karla Ruoco

Render
(Black Balls) Julia Lemos

Music
phenotypo

Client
D&AD

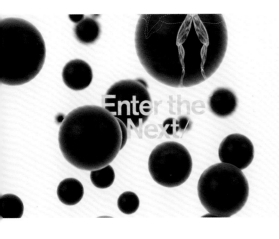

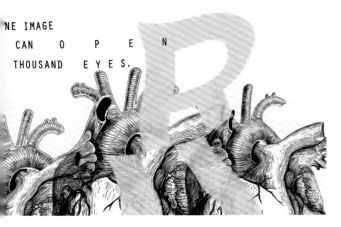
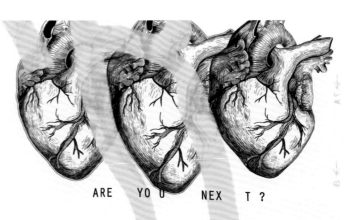

Felipe Frazão made these animations from F/Nazca Saatchi & Saatchi posters for the second edition campaign D&AD "Next Awards." This is a compilation from pieces that were done separately for instagram.

Vimeo

▶ Olympics Medal Tracker

by Illo

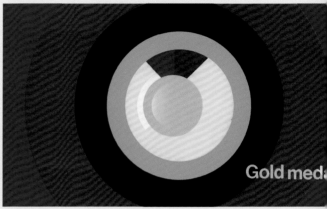

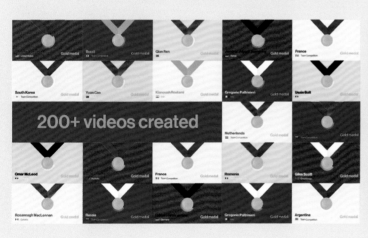

Direction & Animation
Luca Gonnelli

Direction & Design
Ilenia Notarangelo

Coding
Matteo Ruffinengo

Design
Cristina Pasquale

Flags Hero
Miriam Palopoli,
Arianna Cristiano

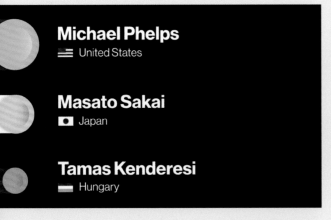

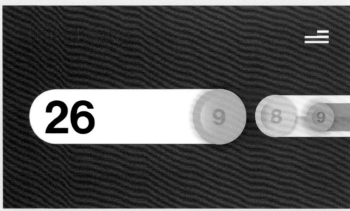

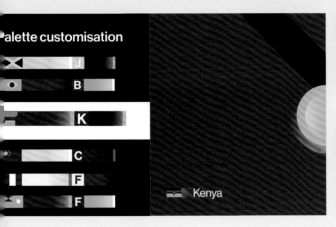

illo.tv/olympics|

Illo developed a platform that is able to automatically render videos in real time combining live data and handmade design templates. They call this "Algo." Partnered with Bloomberg, they used this template and built for them a video medal tracker for the Olympic Games in Rio 2016. Every time when there is a new medal winner, they pulled the fresh data about the sport discipline, the medallists, and the countries' global ranking. Moreover, they customised the template so that it can pick for each sport the appropriate illustration (among around 40 possibilities) and colour palette (one for each of the +200 countries). Then, the video gets rendered in the cloud in a couple of minutes, and becomes available into the Bloomberg infrastructure for publishing.

Vimeo   **Official**

▶ TEDxTaipei 2014 — What Matters Now

by Chu-Chieh Lee

Production
Bito

Direction
Keng-Ming Liu

Design
Chu-Chieh Lee

Production
Oskar Lin

Assistant Production
Manning Lee

Lead Animation
Chu-Chieh Lee

Cel Animation
Guei-Teng Shiu, Sylvia Hsu,
Chu-Chieh Lee,
Kevin Cheng, Hao Yi Chen

2D Animation
Bruce Chen, Chu-Chieh Lee,
Kevin Cheng

3D Animation
Sylvia Hsu

Music
Liya Huang

SFX
David Dunlap

This video is made for TEDxTaipei 2014. The video begins with ocean wave motion, represents the six sub-themes of "What Matters Now," and assembles itself into the Chinese Characters of the theme in negative space, making an intelligent conversion between two languages that challenges the audiences with the effect of optical illusions. It implies that there are usually more than one kind of problems and solutions depending on the viewer's perspective and interpretation. The combination of the eastern and western typefaces also symbolizes the massive changes and influences that TED has experienced in the Chinese society.

Vimeo   Official

▶ Samsung 837 — Tech NYC

by Jonathan Kim

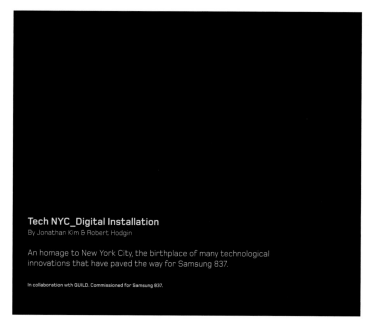

Tech NYC_Digital Installation
By Jonathan Kim & Robert Hodgin

An homage to New York City, the birthplace of many technological
innovations that have paved the way for Samsung 837.

In collaboration wth GUILD. Commissioned for Samsung 837.

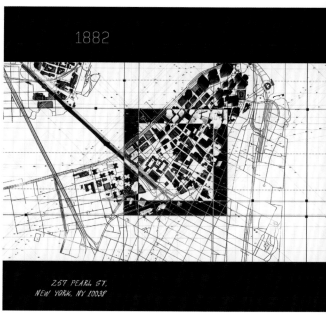

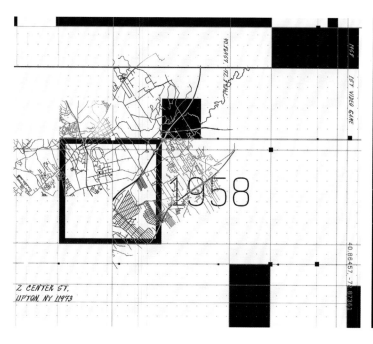

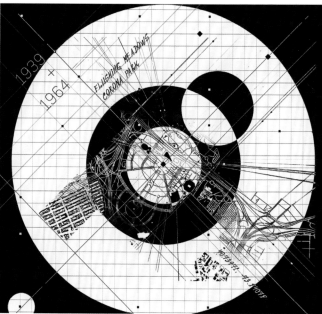

Production
Rare Volume

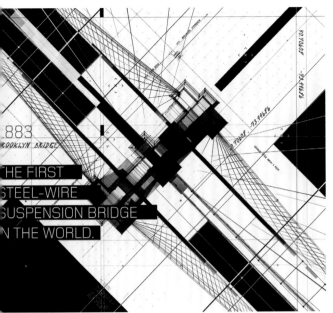

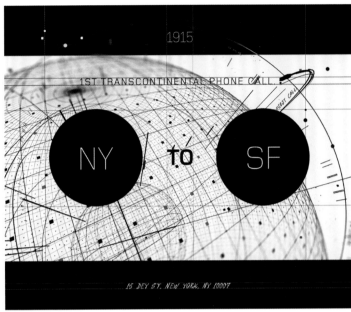

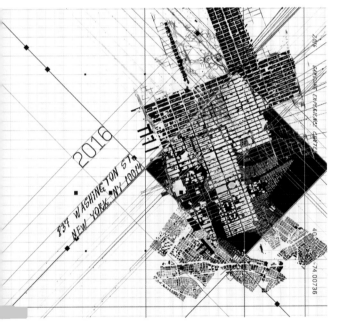

Tech NYC is a design film that outlines technological innovations that have occurred in New York. The final piece is showcased at the Samsung 837 store in Manhattan on a 3-story installation screen.

Vimeo   **Official**

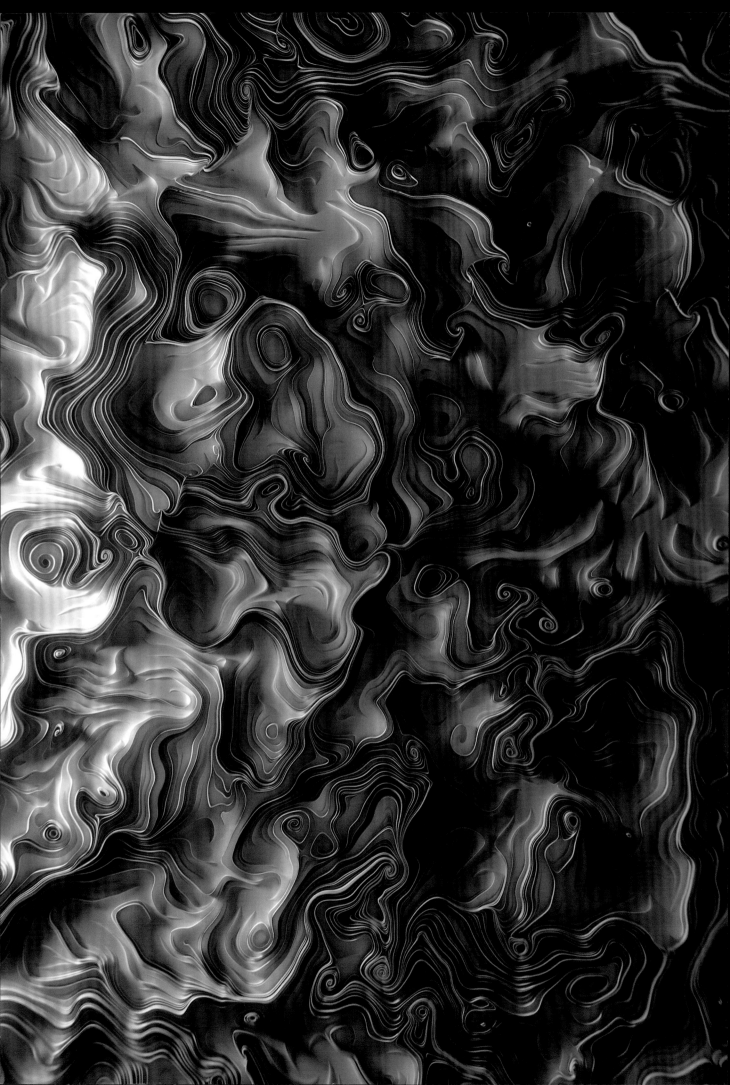

Experimental

▶ Organic Machines Title Sequence

by Xiaolin Zeng

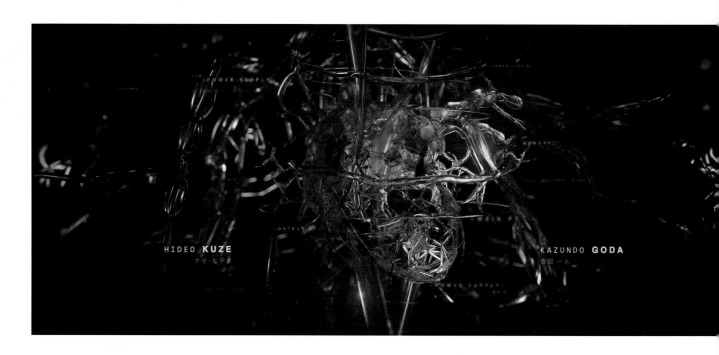

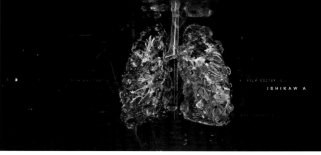

Music
Michael Christian Durrant

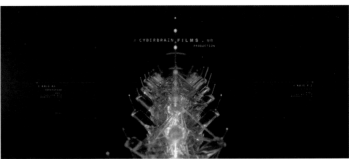

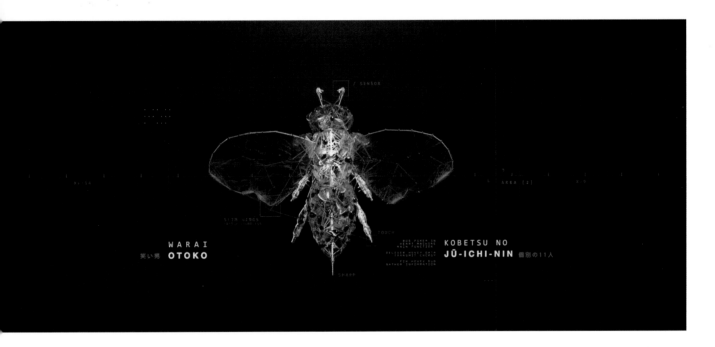

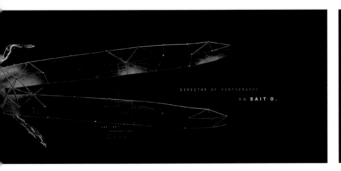

Organic Machines Title Sequence is a spectacular self-initiated title sequence by Chinese designer Xiaolin Zeng (aka. zaoeyo), with credit names borrowed from the characters of Ghost in the Shell. The video mesmerises one man tour-de-force within thoughtful details and shimmering refraction. The designer tries to combine liquid-like machine with human organs. The tiny insects are created as the workers who maintain the machine's functions.

Vimeo   **Official**

▶ Division and Unity
by Territory Studio

Client
ODD NY

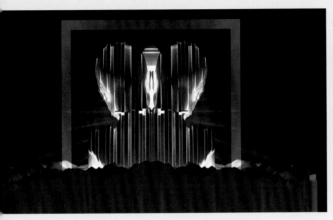

Commissioned to creatively explore the notion of "division" through motion graphics, Territory's response was a collaborative effort in which the very reflections and values of the studio team were articulated as a visual and voice over narrative. Tapping into the studio's collective passion for strong graphic design, richly textured visualisations and storytelling, the animation is a dynamic and thoughtful comment on how the digital age has shaped and influenced us, has led to troubling rifts and divisions across the globe, and how working together makes us stronger.

Vimeo   **Official**

▶ Metrics

by Michael Rigley

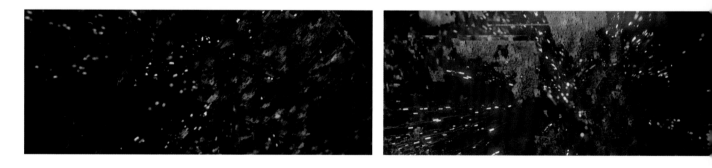

Client
Learn Squared

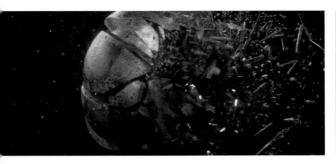
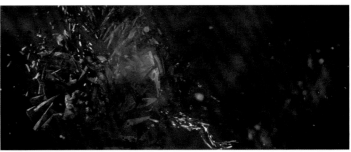

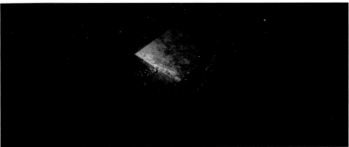

Metric is a design example created for Design for Production training series. It acts as a formal study of both design and process, following the creative brief and curriculum outlined in the course. The class asks students to design a concept around three key words: Volume, Density and Mass. The most recent release in the series walks through the production process of this project and it will help students improve their still concepts into animation.

Vimeo   **Official**

▶ When to the sessions of sweet silent thought

by Taehoon Park

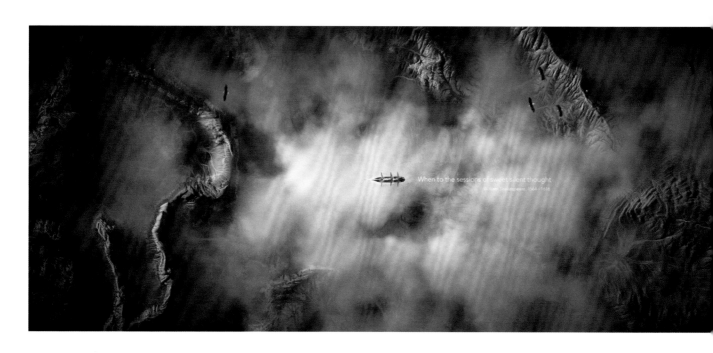

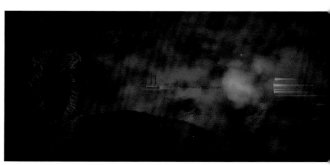

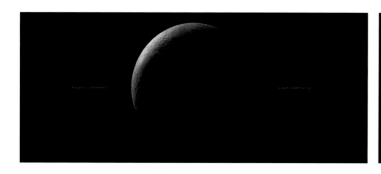

▶ When to the sessions of sweet silent thought

by Taehoon Park

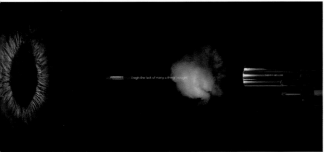 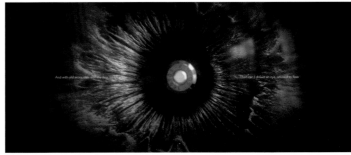

"When to the sessions of sweet silent thought" is a personal project using William Shakespeare's poem. This piece is not only a self-training, but also homage to Patrick Clair's titles sequence. Taehoon Park tried to approach his way of transition for this project.

Vimeo   **Official**

▶ Our Fractal Brains

by Julius Horsthuis

Music
Patrick O'hearn

"When they look at their world they search for patterns, struggling to make sense of a senseless place.

Peace is found in chaos as they fill it with purpose. Connections create meaning in their Fractal Brains."

"Our Fractal Brains" is an experimental motion graphics by Julius Horsthuis to exercise in framing, composition, typography, colour, and style.

Vimeo   **Official**

► Light Matter

by Julius Horsthuis

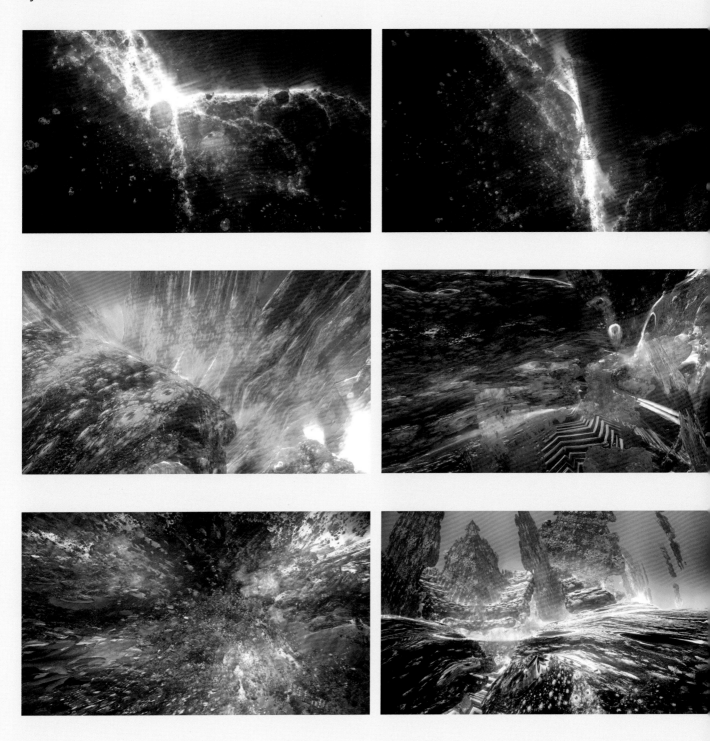

Music
L. Subramaniam

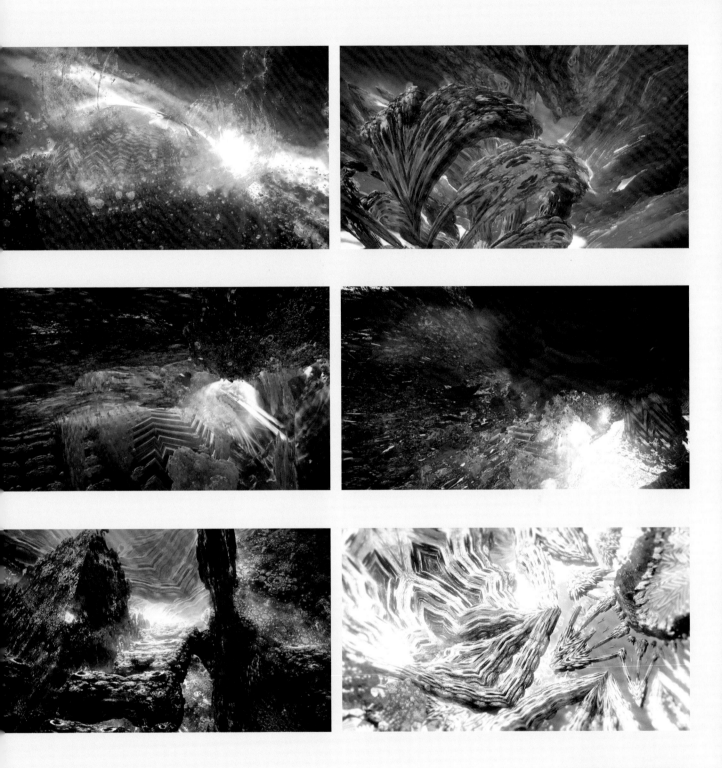

Julius Horsthuis designed this experimental film to convey a
feel that the universe is composed of light matter.

Vimeo   **Official**

▶ Hard Problem of Consciousness

by Julius Horsthuis

Music
Michael Stearns

Consciousness is still a very difficult thing to understand, but it is known that it is linked with the trillions of connections in our brains — our fractal brains. Because the grey matter has developed in a similar way as these visuals: very simple beginnings bring forth infinite complexity.

Vimeo   **Official**

▶ Genesis

by Philat Matveev

In this project, Philat Matveev shares his thoughts of the birth of great ideas and their source on the scale which is overwhelmed by the beam of light, so as to develop an innovative world in a sustainable way.

Vimeo   **Official**

▶ Maxon / Cineversity Ident

by Ranger & Fox

Design
Brett Morris, Steven Panicara

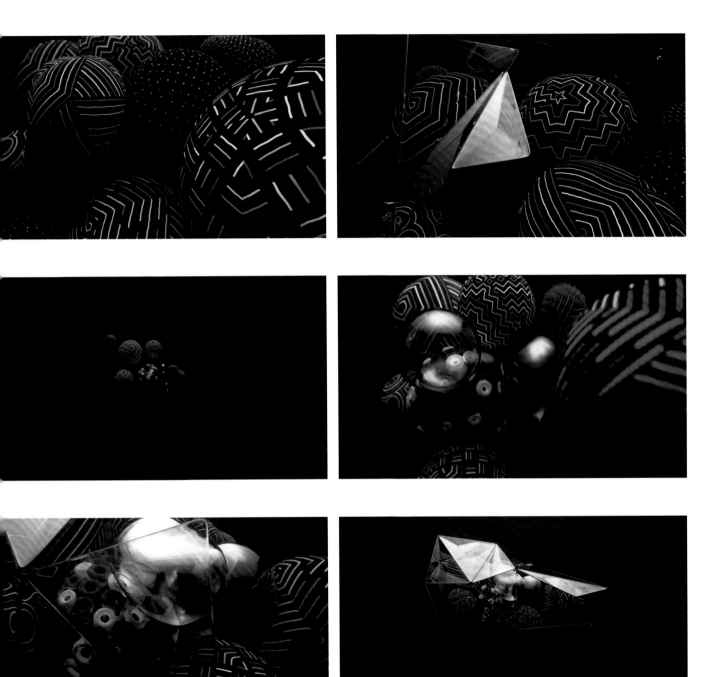

This conceptual thread of the identification was to showcase a range of unique visual styles and techniques which are all used with native cinema 4D tools and rendered. Focusing on the play button of the Cineversity logo, the designers show a progression of abstract styles that transforms more complex visually and technically as the identification progresses, finding brief moments of each style before pulling out to reveal the Cineversity logo encapsulating all the possibilities.

Vimeo   **Official**

▶ An Exit

by Martino Prendini

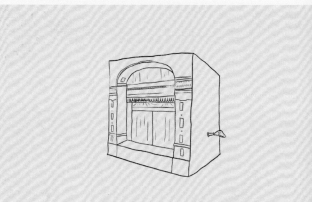

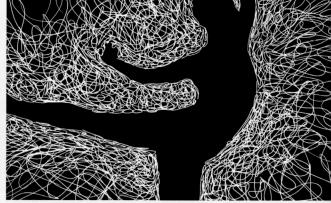
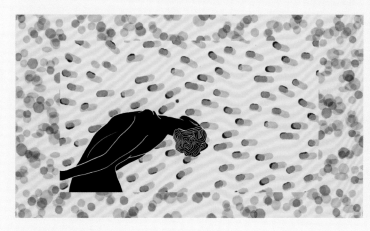

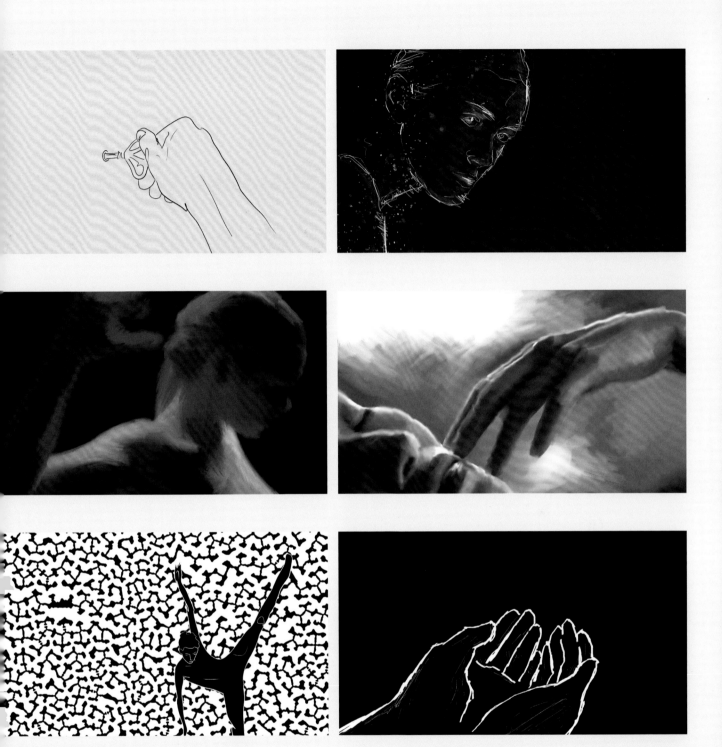

The video is composed of over 6000 images hand-drawn one by one, without being elaborated with glitch and mixed techniques.

It is a project about the constrictive role of women in our society, constantly confined to roles and forced to prove their strength. At the same time, it wants to portray the inner force of female body and emotionality, through an emotional tension that becomes physical.

Vimeo   **Official**

► THE PROCESS

by Salman Sajun

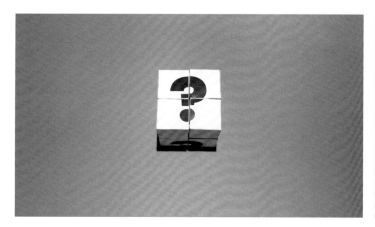

**Direction &
Visual Concept**
Salman Sajun

Art Direction
Sarah Oueller

**Lead Stop-Motion
Animation**
Anna Berezowsky

Paper Props Specialist
Pauline Loctin

Stop-Motion Animation
Laura Stewart

**Stop-Motion Animation &
Art Department**
Raquel Sancinett

**Carpenter & Art
Department**
Filipp Goussevi

Editing
Simon Huang

Sound Design
Mattia
Cellotto

**Motion Control
Equipment**
Kessler Crane

Location
Nomad Nation

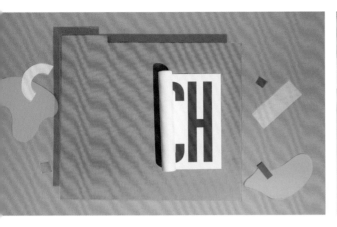

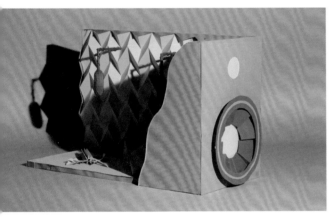
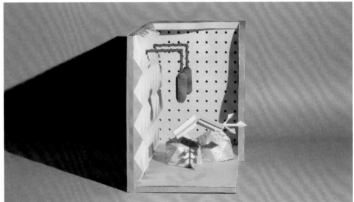

The materials in this film are completely hand-crafted by Slaman Sajun.

The A–Z of creating is a project with truly talented band of magicians. Salman Sajun wanted to show all the different steps involved in the creation process while adding an explosion of colour and wackiness to it all. And everything is shot in camera frame by frame with the magic of stop-motion.

Vimeo　　　　**Official**

▶ A Dusty World
by Jiaqi Wang

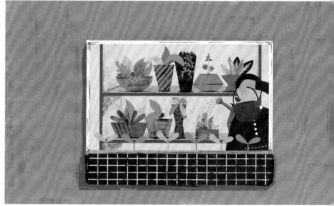

Direction & Animation
Jiaqi Wang

Sound
Matthew Barr

Music
Yosi Horikawa

Note
Screening on Ouchy Film Awards;
12th Athens Animfest;
Anifilm 2017

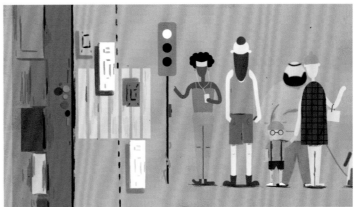

This is a world made by dust, and small group of people live in those dusty pots. A gardener wants to clean those pots, yet destroys the world by accident. This film aims to convey such an idea that any tiny action would make a big difference to our world, disregarding it is either bad or good. However, we ought to take it prudently as the road to hell is paved with good intentions.

Vimeo   **Official**

▶ Art is Theft

by Daniel Moreno Cordero

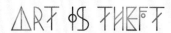

Script, Design & Animation
Daniel Moreno Cordero

Sound & Music Design
Ambrose Yu

Voice Over Artist
Bob Bavnani

Script Supervision & Social Media
Evan Brown

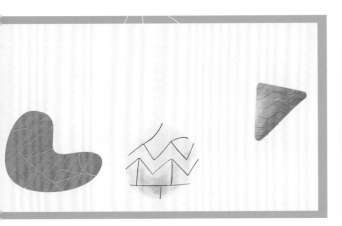

GOOD ARTISTS COPY:
GREAT ARTISTS STEAL

Creation is not inspired by one man, woman or one thing. Artists are influenced by people's daily affair, diverse artists, etc. With this film, Daniel Cordero attempted to convey an approach to the creative process and express how all artists, at any level, "steal" the art and the very soul of other artists, while forming their "original" pieces.

Daniel made plenty of references to his favourite artists, such as the geometric and free style forms, which are a salute to Ancient Hellenic Art, Picasso's experimental sculptures, Japanese animations, and more.

Vimeo **Official**

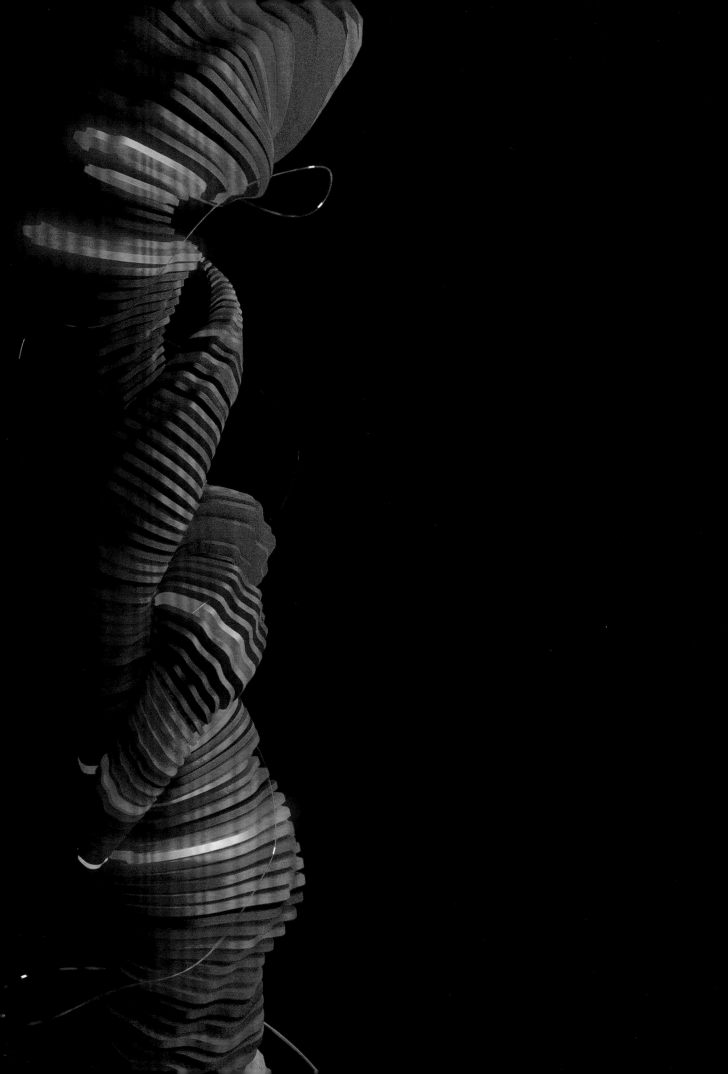

Title Sequence

► Lomonosov

by Grad Studio

 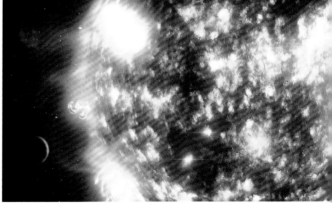

Direction
Alexey Denisov

CG Direction
Vlad Tkachuk

Production
Vasily Yakovlev

CG Supervision
Evgeny Chebotar

CG Art
Evgeny Kolesnikov,
Vadim Ermakov

In-house Direction
Vlad Tkachuk

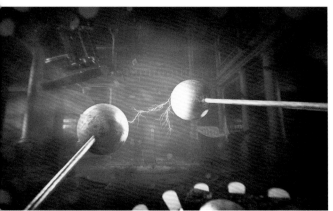

Grad Studio designed this film for a documentary about Mikhail Lomonosov, who is regarded as one of the greatest Russian scientists living in around 1700.

The time goes back fleetly into the past and the designers plunge into the world of the brilliant mind. He was a genius of astronomy, physics, chemistry, philology, mosaic art, natural history, and poetry. Floating through the air, the objects recreate the achievements and discoveries of the first Russian scientist.

Vimeo   **Official**

▶ NEXTSOUND 2016

by Eugene Pylinsky

Music
Mouse on Mars

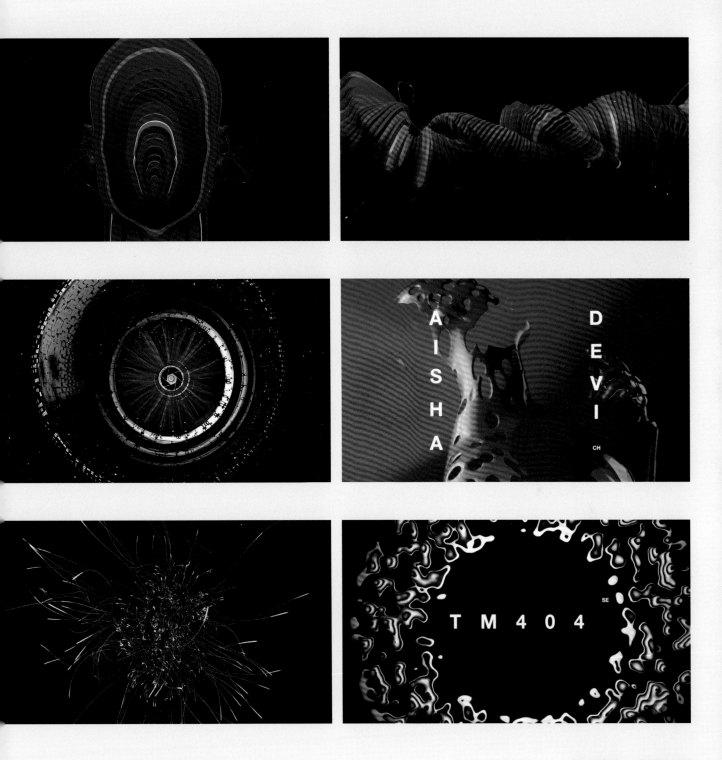

This title was created for the 4th annual progressive music and digital art festival NEXTSOUND. The main idea was to show how music affects people, and transfers them from pretty normal states to incredible stages.

Vimeo   **Official**

▶ SXSW Gaming Awards 2017

by Imaginary Forces

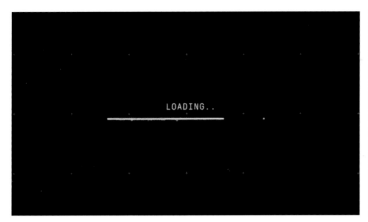
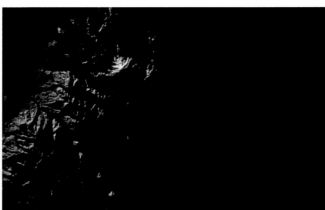

Creative Direction
Jeremy Cox

Art Direction
Max Strizich

Executive Production
Jon Hassell

Head of Production
Aleen Kim

Design
Jeremy Cox, Max Strizich,
Amy Wallace

3D Animation
Jeremy Cox, Max Strizich,
Hogan Williams, Henry Chang,
Paolo Cogliati

2D Animation
Nathan Goodell, Isabell Hacker,
Daniel Blanco

Editing
Rachel Ambelang

Audio
Nacwin Music

Client
SXSW GAMING

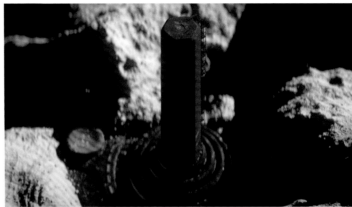

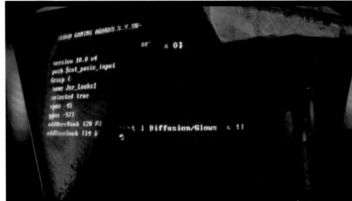

The SXSW Gaming Awards have been an amazing opportunity to explore and try new things. For the titles for 2017, Imaginary Forces started with gaming hardware, added a big slice of NASA space photography, a dash of retro sci-fi book covers, and a pinch of *2001: A Space Odyssey*. The designers combined them together into an opening that transports the audience into the world of the SXSW Gaming Awards.

Vimeo   **Official**

▶ Mirage Festival 2017

by nöbl.tv

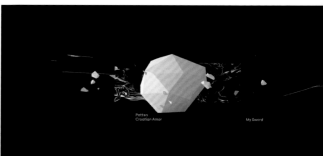

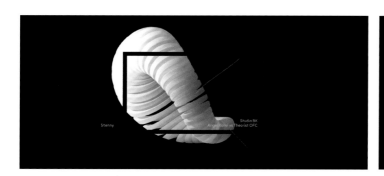

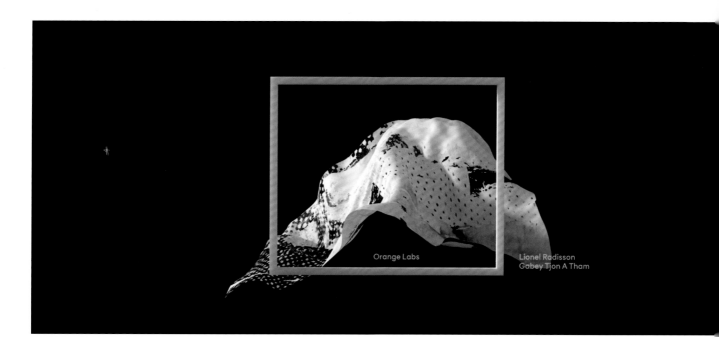

Direction & Animation
nöbl

Design
Cyril Izarn, Julien Nantiec

Additional Design
DXMIQ, Arnaud Laffond

Music
Sebastian Oliwa

Client
Mirage Festival

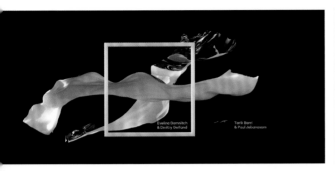

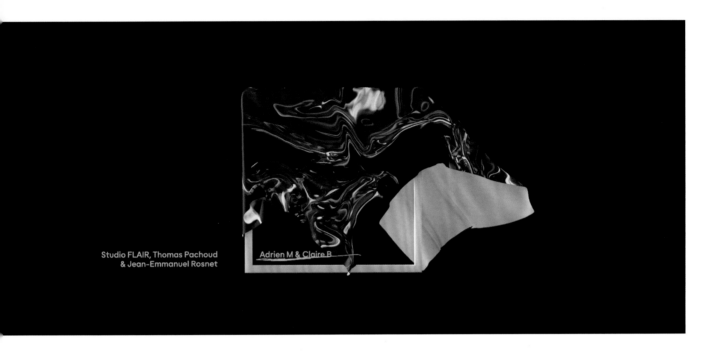

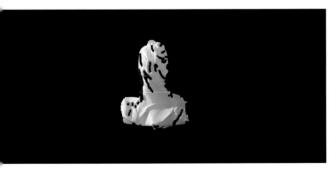

The opening titles for the 5th edition of Mirage festival, an event that highlights many artists from various disciplines like art, innovation, and digital culture, are an experimentation inspired by digital art installations and explore different kind of shapes, waves, and textures.

Special thanks to DXMIQ and Arnaud Laffond for their precious help.

Vimeo   **Official**

▶ Da Vinci's Demons

by Huge Designs

Design & Composition
Paul McDonnell

Illustration
Nathan McKenna

Art Direction
Hugo Moss

NOTE
Winner of Creative Arts
Emmy Awards 2013 —
Main Title Design

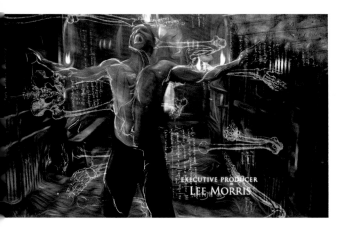

Da Vinci's Demons fictionalised the early days of Leonardo Da Vinci — the very well-known multidisciplinary genius as an artist, inventor, and dreamer — about his feverish ambitions to change the future.

The thorough illustrative style infuses artistic feel into this historical drama with abundant details, making a consistent look with the master's hand-scripts and evoking a fancy narrative. Moreover, the music was a key part of the sequence to symbolise Da Vinci's mirroring notes, and therefore it is palindromic — play forward is the same as play backward.

Vimeo   **Official**

▶ The Shannara Chronicles

by Huge Designs

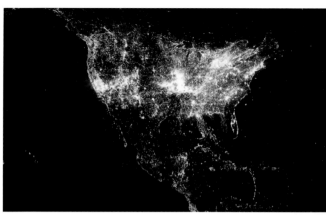

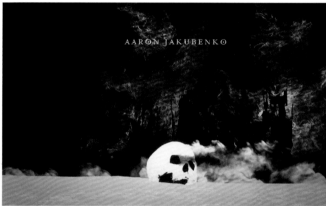

Design
Paul McDonnell

Art Direction
Hugo Moss

Composition
Paul McDonnell

3D Design
Ben Hanbury

NOTE
Official selection for
SXSW 2016

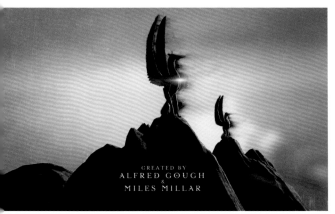

Based on the best-selling fantasy book series by Terry Brooks, "The Shannara Chronicles" follows heroes in the Four Lands as they embark on a quest to stop an evil Demon army from destroying the universe.

In a short space of time, the opening title had to tell the story of how the world recovered from the end of civilization as they know it, to the rise of the Elves, Gnomes, Dwarves and Trolls.

Vimeo   **Official**

▶ Jules Unlimited

by Floris Vos

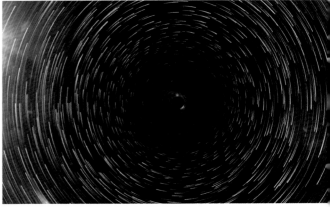
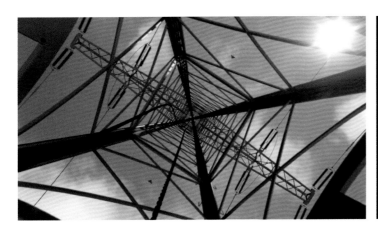

Creative Partner
Menno Wisselink

3D Production
Michael Visser

3D Art
Andre Ferwerda

Music & Sound Design
Studio Takt

Client
VARA (Marijtje van Amersvoort)

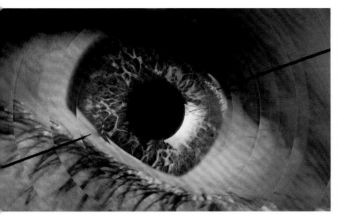
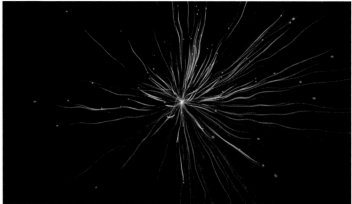

Dutch national broadcaster VARA decided to bring back
a long gone popular science TV series — a new series of
adventures, science, and experiences. Their main contents are
Perspective, Immersion, Experience, and Science.

Vimeo   **Official**

▶ Outpost
by Imaginary Forces

Creative Direction
Tosh Kodama

Executive Production
Chris Hill

Head of Production
Franceska Bucci

Production
Maggie Robinson

Design
Craig Stouffer, Arisu Kashiwagi

Animation
Jahmad Rollins, Daesun Hwang,
Kathy Liang, Freddy Morales,
David Orwasky

Editing
Bryan Keith

Client
Univision / HBO

Created by Eric Douat and Juan Rendon, and executive produced by Pharrell Williams and Mimi Valdes, Outpost is a series which showcases different global causes and multicultural perspectives. The main title created by CD Tosh Kodama captures the raw energy of a series which takes the viewer around the globe exploring the unexpected and overlooked stories of our generation.

Vimeo   Official

▶ Dos Lunas

by Frame

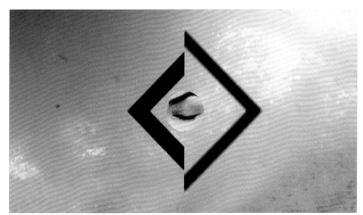

Creative Direction
Anders Schroder

Brand Direction
Peter Liljenberg

Design
Santiago Zoraidez, FOX

Executive Production
Thomas Bay

Animation
Tom Crate,
Franz Ferdinand Kubin

Client
FOX International Channels
Latin America

Fox International Channels chose Frame for the design and production of their latest original series program package.

The new series, titled Dos Lunas (Two Moons in Spanish), centers on a split personality character, played by Bárbara Mori — one of the biggest female stars in Latin America.

Frame wanted to visualise the opposing character traits by juxtaposing the sensual with the psychological, using close-up studies of the human body and connect it all with splitting shapes, asymmetric wipes, and strong symbols.

Vimeo   **Official**

▶ Underground: Main Titles

by Imaginary Forces

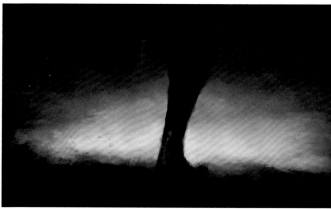
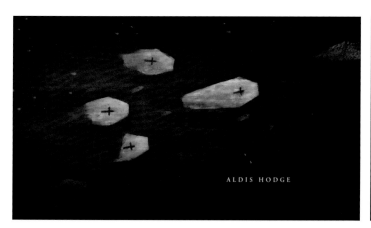
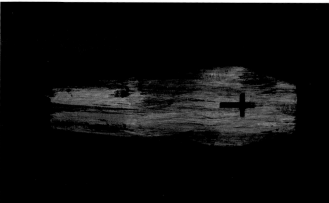

Creative Direction
Dan Gregoras

Executive Production
Jon Hassell

Associate Production
Tess Sitzmann

Art Direction
Max Strizich

2D Animation
Max Strizich, Mark Thompson,
Cyprian Sadlon, Tim Beckhardt

Additional Designs
Theo Daley, Jeremy Cox

Coordination
Krista Templeton

Storyboard Art
Chris Wolfgang Mauch

Illustration
Victoria Allen

Concept Design
Victoria Allen

Production Assistant
Ruth Estrada

Client
WGN

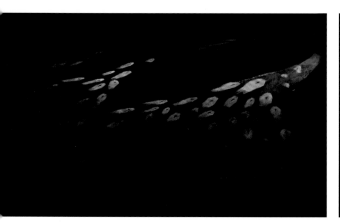
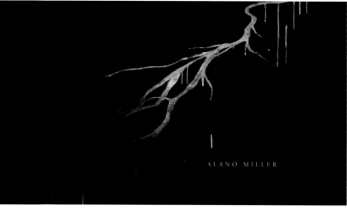

WGN America's Underground took America by storm as the network's most-watched original scripted entertainment program. Underground is a secret route and shelter in nineteenth century America. African-American slaves used it to flee to the free states and Canada. Producer John Legend strived to make audiences feel the stories are alive instead of like paintings hanging on a wall in a museum. To reflect this, Imaginary Forces depicted a man fleeing for days and nights in the underground, climbing over mountains and escaping from wolves. They subtly conveyed the theme of this drama — to struggle with a life time to be free — as the man running into a beam of light at the end of the sequence, which is also a perfect timing for the beginning of the show.

Vimeo   **Official**

▶ By Any Means

by Huge Designs

Design & Composition
Paul McDonnell

**Art Direction &
Live Action Direction**
Hugo Moss

NOTE
Nominated for an RTS Award
2014

By Any Means follows a clandestine unit living on the edge and playing the criminal elite at their own game, existing in the grey area between the letter of the law and true justice.

The opening titles are a mixture of filmed elements blended with 3D graphics. The sequence consists of a constantly turning line between black and white, good and evil. The line continuously evolves whilst the narrative of a criminal being pursued, caught and imprisoned is played out in a visually arresting way.

Vimeo　　　**Official**

▶ Into the Badlands

by Huge Designs

Design & Composition
Paul McDonnell

Art Direction
Hugo Moss

3D Design
Ben Hanbury

NOTE
Official Selection for
SXSW 2016

A mighty warrior and a young boy search for enlightenment in a ruthless territory controlled by feudal barons.

The opening titles gathered its inspiration from Martial Arts films from the 1970s. It abstractly tells the narrative of an indentured servant trying to break the chains of his lord.

Vimeo　　**Official**

▶ FITC Tokyo 15

by Michael Rigley

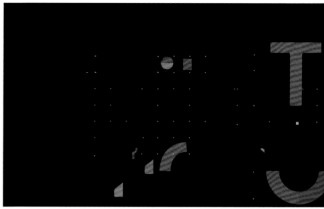
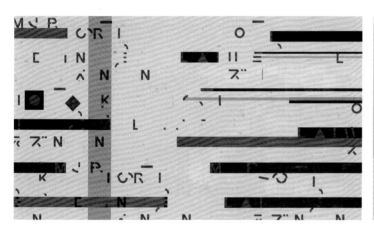
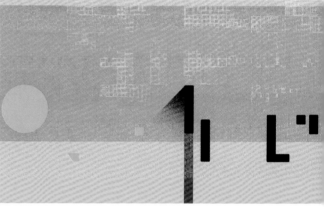
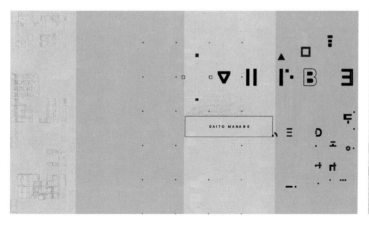
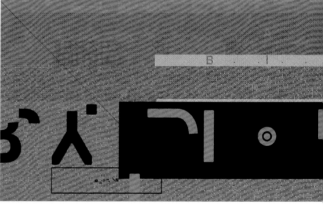

Direction
Ash Thorp

Production
Andrew Hawryluk

Art Direction
Michael Rigley

Type Design
Nicolas Girard

Design
Ash Thorp, Michael Rigley,
Nicolas Girard

Type
Animation Nicolas Girard,
Alasdair Willson

Animation
Michael Rigley, Chris Bjerre,
Andrew Hawryluk

Computational Art
Albert Omoss

Process Reel Editing
Franck Deron

Composition
Pilotpriest

Client
FITC

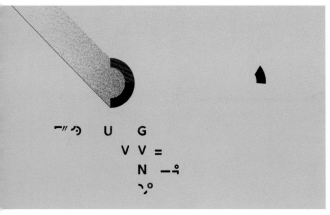
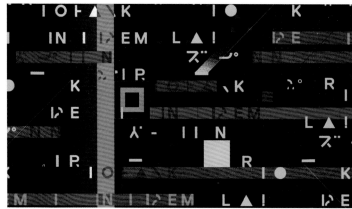
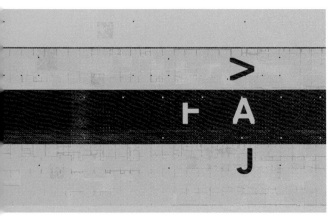

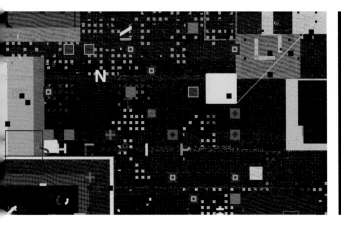
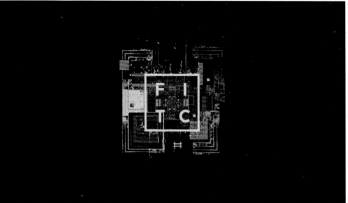

To commemorate FITC Tokyo's inaugural title sequence, the designers sought to encapsulate the city itself — distilled to graphic form. Aiming to contrast the harmonies of traditional Japanese culture against the backdrop and sensory overload of present-day Tokyo, they meticulously crafted elegant typographic forms to collide with abrasive, overstimulating glitch — giving way to a progressive journey where moments of extreme chaos fold into temporary tranquillity.

Vimeo   **Official**

▶ SBS Special

by MAINCONCEPT

Direction & Design
Taiho Roh

This project is a documentary opening titles sequence for the SBS channel in Korea. It is a journey to find traces of Korea in Japan, showing the historical and cultural connection of Korea and Japan that the ordinary did not know.

Vimeo   **Official**

Index

4HUMANS

http://www.4humans.tv

4HUMANS is a multi-lingual and multi-platform production company specializing in building memorable audiovisual experiences. They create top-notch animations and unusual live action. They develop incredible characters and unique worlds. They produce fluffy emotions, colour palettes, and sunny smiles. Their mission is to connect humans in a fun and friendly way, using a wide range of techniques, from stop motion to VR.

P026 – 027; P056 – 057; P154 – 155

Alex Frukta

https://www.behance.net/mrfrukta

Born in 1992 in Saint Petersburg, Alex Frukta is a designer specializing in motion, illustration, and typography. He is also the co-founder of NORD Collective, and a member of Designcollector team.

P068 – 069; P072 – 073; P164 – 165; P166 – 167

ALLd. inc.

http://alld.jp

OLD ≠ ALLd.

ALLd. inc. is a motion design company based in Japan. The creative company focuses on movie and graphics mainly with motion graphics. They've been pursuing video and design which are steadfast flame by flame and never get old even if time passes.

P158 – 159; P160 – 161

Block & Tackle

http://www.blockandtackle.tv

Block & Tackle is an award-winning and design-driven production company focused on visual storytelling through animation, live-action, stop-motion, or any means necessary.

P058 – 059

Chu-Chieh Lee

https://chuchiehlee.com

Chu-Chieh Lee is a designer and animator from Taiwan.

She is a multi-disciplinary motion graphic designer currently working as a freelancer. She always has a great passion for motion graphics, and for creating, drawing, and adding beauty to her life and projects she works on. Driven by endless curiosity and inspired by daily life, she enjoys using different media to challenge herself and explore different styles in her work.

P040 – 041; P066 – 067; P172 – 173

Clemens Wirth

http://www.clemenswirth.com

Living in Innsbruck, Austria, Clemens Wirth is a director, motion designer and animator with a passion for macro photography, model building and titles design.

P150 – 151

Cobb Studio

http://cobb.tv

Wonseok Lee, the founder of Cobb Studio, is a motion graphic designer who has been working with major Broadcasting Stations (KBS2, MBC, JTBC, SBS) and companies (Samsung, LG, Hyundae, Olleh) in Korea for the past 10 years. He groups together with designers who love animals and animation in Cobb Studio.

P048 – 049; P118 – 119

Daniel Moreno Cordero

http://www.danielcordero.net

Born in 1981 in Cádiz, Spain, Daniel Moreno Cordero is a freelance designer specializing in graphic design, editorial layout, motion graphics, video, VFX, animation, and illustration for companies.

P064 – 065; P106 – 107; P202 – 203

Ditroit

http://ditroit.it

Consisting of a team of passionate art directors, designers, and animators, Ditroit is an award winning motion studio based in Milan and London, producing creative motion design content for international brands, TV networks and advertising agencies. They love to create engaging visual experiences and receive challenging briefs.

P018 – 019; P036 – 037; P046 – 047; P060 – 061

Eugene Pylinsky

https://epylinsky.myportfolio.com

Eugene Pylinsky is a freelance motion graphics artist based in Kyiv, Ukraine.

P086 – 087; P088 – 089; P208 – 209

Felipe Frazão

http://www.fraza.com.br

Passionate for making and crafting things in the physical world, Felipe Frazão is a Brazilian motion designer and generalist.

P098 – 099; P102 – 103; P168 – 169

Floris Vos

http://www.florisvos.com

With his images and sounds, Floris Vos tells stories, creates experiences, and sets moods which are stylized, surreal, and sometimes heavily drained in abstraction and metaphorical imagery. He always tries to find the balance between commissioned work and art projects. He is constantly developing new styles, different techniques, and new perspectives for narrative. From concept to delivery, he strives to consistently produce work that is visceral, innovative and diverse.

P218 – 219

Frame

https://frame.dk

Frame is an award-winning motion design studio located in the cold north of Denmark. With an international client base, and as the largest studio in Denmark, they make all kinds of clever stuff for screens of all sizes, be it commercials, broadcast promotions, films and digital projects.

They always strive to be diverse. Made up of talented designers, animators, directors and producers, the team use a wide range of skills help bring brands to life from original idea to final product.

P020 – 021; P044 – 045; P082 – 083; P222 – 223

Goodbye Kansas

http://goodbyekansas.com

Goodbye Kansas is a Scandinavian VFX house with a strong focus on animation and VFX. The company is based in Sweden, with offices and studios in Hamburg and London.

The studio aims to be intimately associated with the most iconic characters and stories of popular culture by pure force of imagination and technical excellence. Their award-winning wizards in VFX, CGI, motion capture and animations have played a role in TV, movies, game trailers, and commercials that define popular culture all over the world.

P024 – 025; P032 – 033

Grad Studio

http://www.cinemagrad.com

Grad Studio is one of the top three Russian companies regarding advertising and documentary post-production. The studio is ready to create CG of any level of difficulties. The crews have accumulated experience of creating projects from Demo, from parts to Full CGI, to shots of characters with photo-realistic quality.

P206 – 207

Huge Designs

http://hugedesigns.co.uk

Based in central London, Huge Designs is an Emmy award winning titles design company. It was founded by Hugo Moss in a single room in the basement of an office in Soho, London. Later, it becomes a notable studio with over 300 television credited to its name. They have been acknowledged with many awards, including Emmy Awards and Royal Television Society Award.

P214 – 215; P216 – 217; P226 – 227; P228 – 229

Illo

https://illo.tv

ILLO is a design and animation driven studio based in Italy, co-founded by Ilenia Notarangelo and Luca Gonnelli — partners and directors. They currently lead a gang of 11 designers, animators, coders and a french bulldog named Pinguino (literally, Penguin).

The studio's primary focus is simplifying technology by invading the world with colourful geometric motion graphics or live action set design.

They recently created Algo, an automated video engine that can transform live data into motion design videos that can be called "self-driving videos."

P050 – 051; P054 – 055; P170 – 171

Imaginary Forces

https://www.imaginaryforces.com

Imaginary Forces is a creative company specializing in visual storytelling and brand strategy. With studios in both Los Angeles and New York, Imaginary Forces is powered by talented individuals working together to push the limits of creative possibility. They make design-driven content for a wide range of partners and projects.

INLAND STUDIO

http://www.inlandstudio.tv

INLAND STUDIO is a design and animation company based in Buenos Aires. It produces high impact and solid concept for branding and advertisements, caring deeply for details playing with visual rhythms, reinventing resources, and exposing them in their best. With a compelling 3D team, animations that stands from subtle to strident, and unique design and creative direction, INLAND has made its way as one of the most solid studios in the Argentinean emerging animation scene.

Jhao-Yu Shih

http://littleoil.tumblr.com

Jhao-Yu Shih was born in Taichung City, Taiwan. She is working in Taiwan as a freelance designer and manages her own illustration brand "Little Oil" for publishing, animation, and music agency.

She graduated with FA (Hons) in Visual Communication from Shih-Chien University, Taipei, and was employed as an artist in Sofa Studio in Taipei as well. Her works involve pre-production design, story concept design, character design, scene design, and colour script. She is the contributor of several well-known animations, such as "MuMu Hug" and "Monster Coins."

Jiaqi Wang

http://jiaqiwang.org

Jiaqi Wang is an animator and illustrator from China. In 2016, she has completed her MA in Animation at London College of Art. She has screened films in international film festivals. Specializing in 2D moving images and motion graphics. Her work revolves imagination about daily life, full of colours, visual design, and character design.

John Christian Ferner Apalnes

http://www.isawjohnfirst.com

John Christian Ferner Apalnes works across animation, live action, sound, music, drawing, model making, sculpting, and 3D design and compositing. Scenes, characters, textures, moods, staged environments and surreal and artificial memory logic operate as tools for his continuous exploring of strange territories.

Jonathan Kim

http://jonathankim.work

Jonathan Kim is a creative director and partner at Rare Volume, which is a design studio based in New York. Rare Volume specializes in motion design, creative code, and interactive installations. He has been partnering up with some of the industry's top agencies and brands to craft award-winning experiences for Nike, Disney, Toyota, Audible, Pepsi, and Samsung.

Julius Horsthuis

http://www.julius-horsthuis.com

Julius Horsthuis is a VFX supervisor working at Hectic Electric, a creative post production house based in Amsterdam, and also a fractal artist.

Le Cube

http://lecube.tv

Le Cube is a design studio based in Buenos Aires and São Paulo, working for clients in the worldwide. The team is composed of a crew of crazy sailors that strive to produce promising and honourable results.

Loop

http://the-loop.tv

Loop is a design and animation studio founded in 2014 by a collective of experienced artists who are constantly pushing their limits to reach new goals and rise to the new levels. By gathering best talents into one well-organized team, they are constantly growing, exploring new design fields, styles, and techniques to achieve best results, and providing the most incredible visual solutions of any kind.

Their clients include Boeing, Bloomberg, New Balance, Samsung, to name just a few. In the meantime, they are also collaborating with the best agencies, production, and postproduction companies from all over the world.

P012 – 013; P022 – 023; P144 – 145

LUMBRE

http://www.lumbre.tv

LUMBRE is a multi-disciplinary studio and branding consultancy that specializes in entertainment and television. They offer creative solutions to clients across the globe. They use their expertise in visual storytelling to bring brands to life in authentic and original ways. They work closely with their clients with tailored creations not only for their operational and commercial needs, but also to capture the identity of the brand. By finding the core truth of what differentiates the brand, they create a story that conveys it in an unforgettable way to its audience.

P112 – 113

MAINCONCEPT

http://www.mainconcep-t.com

MAINCONCEPT is a design studio based in Seoul. The multidisciplinary studio works across different area like art, digital media, and branding production.

P028 – 029; P232

Martino Prendini

http://martinoprendini.com

Martino Prendini lives in Rovigo, Italy, and works mainly as an illustrator. His creative path starts with graphic design and meets different visual media, from music videos to animation, from glitch art to live visuals.

P196 – 197

Michael Rigley

http://michaelrigley.com

Michael Rigley is an award-winning art director and designer. His work spans multiple disciplines, from film, broadcast and gaming, to virtual reality, live visuals and real-time graphics. He is also an instructor at Learn Squared, developing original course content, and teaching alongside industry-leading creatives.

P182 – 183; P230 – 231

Mikhail Sedov

http://subframestudio.com

Mikhail Sedov is an art director and motion artist based in Moscow, Russia.

P038 – 039

MixCode

http://mixcode.tv

MixCode, officially founded in 2014, is a professional team working on visual art, especially animation and motion graphics. Born with overflowing energy, they keep creating enchanting stories and eyes-catching works. Their team have gained second price of 2015 Young Director Awards and joined 2015 Vivid Sydney. They are always curious, humorous, and energetic. They always create works that bring their audiences Wow!

P108 – 109; P116 – 117

nöbl.tv

http://www.nobl.tv

nöbl.tv is a French design and motion studio founded by Julien Nantiec and Cyril Izarn. They craft complete universes for broadcasting, digital, and events. With multidisciplinary thinking, they focus on art direction, and they like to express simple and original ideas. They also evolve in several aesthetics and techniques in order to obtain singular renders. To achieve this, they federate the most relevant talents at every step of their projects.

P076 – 077; P124 – 125; P162 – 163; P212 – 213

Ouchhh Studio

http://www.ouchhh.tv

Ouchhh is a creative new media studio with expertise in animation, motion graphics, and public art. With offices in Istanbul and Los Angeles, Ouchhh integrates art, science, and technology in all its work. It is a multidisciplinary creative hub focused on interactive new media platforms, kinetic sculptures, and immersive experiences, offering direction, art direction, and producing video mapping projections. Ouchhh's works have received multiple accolades and awards in the international arena. From show-stopping outdoor A/V performances to groundbreaking graphics creations, Ouchhh considers each project as a challenge, and takes a fresh and unique approach for all of their works. Ouchhh's collaborators transcend all industries and all continents, including Google, CERN, Nike, Cosmopolitan, WIRED, etc.

Panoply

http://www.panoply.co.uk

Panoply is a design and motion studio based in London, UK. Combining their expertise in creative thinking, design-led outcomes, and high-end production, they develop compelling and differentiating works. They craft experiences for advertising, broadcast, digital, and print with projects such as commercials, product campaigns, brand films, on-air rebrands, and many more.

Parallel Teeth

http://parallelteeth.com

Parallel Teeth is the alias of Robert Wallace who is a director, animator and graphic artist. He works across a range of media, including music videos, commercials, album artwork, installations, and murals.

Philat Matveev

https://www.behance.net/philphilphil?

Philat Matveev is a Russian motion graphic designer based in Moscow.

Radugadesign

http://radugadesign.com

Radugadesign is a media design studio based in Moscow, Russia, specializing in motion design, video mapping, and interactive installations. Since 2007, Radugadesign has realized more than 350 unique projects, including international projects in France, Belgium, Korea, CIS, USA, China and even on the North Pole. They provide a unique range of services in multimedia design and technical support for events of any scale: from audio-visual shows to interactive installations. In their projects, they also unite the best professionals: artists, musicians, coders, architects, directors and technical partners.

Ranger & Fox

http://rangerandfox.tv

Ranger & Fox is a newly formed studio helmed by Brett Morris and Steve Panicara. They specialize in discovery, strategy, and visual communication. Ranger & Fox brings a clever and cunning approach to every project.

Sagnik Sengupta

https://www.behance.net/sagniksengupta

Sagnik Sengupta lives in New Delhi and is currently working as a motion designer for Ten Sports Network India. Started his career as a graphic designer in 2010, he has fell in love with the possibilities of motion design could offer in terms of design and animation and immediately got hooked to it. Some of his works and reels have been featured on different design websites which motivate and push himself to keep on improvement. His creative weapons are Cinema 4d and the Adobe Suit.

Salman Sajun

http://www.salmansajun.com

Salman Sajun is a director who runs a creative studio that specializes in bringing the inanimate to life through a magical blend of stop motion and live action. He has a handpicked team of creative ninjas. They work together to make the world a more colourful and aesthetically pleasing place where imagination runs wild and creativity drives all content.

As a director, he has created dozens of commercials and short films for clients all around the world. Every project is approached with a whimsical curiosity that results in brand-new experience.

P198 – 199

Sébastien Henau

https://www.behance.net/sebastienhenau

Sébastien Henau is a student studying Devine (Digital Design and Development) in Belgium. He is also working as a creative developer and animator at Little Miss Robot Studio.

P074 – 075

Sociedad Fantasma

http://www.sociedadfantasma.com

Sociedad Fantasma is a collaborative story telling studio specializing in animation and illustration. In each of their projects, they work with the best creatives, crafters, and visual artists to create the best experiences for their clients.

P126 – 127

Taehoon Park

https://www.behance.net/pth0427

Based in Seoul, Korea, Taehoon Park works as a 3D artist and motion graphic designer. With a strong passion for titles design, cool looking artwork, short animation, and lighting, he aims to be an art director.

P184 – 185

Territory Studio

http://www.territorystudio.com

Territory Studio brings deep expertise of narrative design for film, games, and brands, and what ties their work together is a love of craft and creative, a passion for storytelling, and a designer's eye for problem solving. Their uniquely refined design intelligence, near-future expertise, and a team of ambitious, focused and proactive cross-discipline specialists shape the studio distinguishing.

P128 – 129; P180 – 181

Tony Zagoraios

http://www.artonemotion.com

Tony Zagoraios is an award-winning and innovative motion designer and director. As a self-taught designer, Tony had the chance to develop a unique, sharp, and, to some extent, experimental style that is evident in most of his works. Fearless to swim in uncharted waters, he manages to discover fresh styles and be one step ahead at all times.

P084 – 085

Troublemakers

http://troublemakers.tv

Founded in 2008, Troublemakers.tv is a production company and studio based in the heart of Paris. Their producers and directors are united by a common love for design, an unending curiosity, an unwavering attention to detail, and a shared joy in the perfection of the pixel.

P090 – 091; P092 – 093

Whitelight Motion

http://whitelightmotion.tv

Whitelight Motion Studio is a hybrid creative studio focusing on expanding the possibilities between motion graphics and video installation.

P094 – 095

Xiaolin Zeng

http://behance.net/zaoeyo

Xiaolin Zeng (aka. Zaoeyo) is a self-taught visual designer who focuses on 3D visuals, motion design, and titles design.

P178 – 179

Acknowledgements

We would like to thank all of the designers involved for granting us permission to publish their works, as well as all of the photographers who have generously allowed us to use their images. We are also very grateful to many other people whose names do not appear in the credits but who made specific contributions and provided support. Without these people, we would not have been able to share these beautiful works with readers around the world. Our editorial team includes editor Javier Zheng and book designer Dingding Huo, to whom we are truly grateful.